CW00394935

Strategic Leadership

Strategic Leadership

How to think and plan strategically and provide direction

JOHN ADAIR

KoganPage

LONDON PHILADELPHIA NEW DELHI

Publisher's note

Every possible effort has been made to ensure that the information contained in this book is accurate at the time of going to press, and the publishers and authors cannot accept responsibility for any errors or omissions, however caused. No responsibility for loss or damage occasioned to any person acting, or refraining from action, as a result of the material in this publication can be accepted by the editor, the publisher or the author.

First published in Great Britain and the United States in 2010 by Kogan Page Limited

Apart from any fair dealing for the purposes of research or private study, or criticism or review, as permitted under the Copyright, Designs and Patents Act 1988, this publication may only be reproduced, stored or transmitted, in any form or by any means, with the prior permission in writing of the publishers, or in the case of reprographic reproduction in accordance with the terms and licences issued by the CLA. Enquiries concerning reproduction outside these terms should be sent to the publishers at the undermentioned addresses:

120 Pentonville Road	525 South 4th Street, #241	4737/23 Ansari Road
London N1 9JN	Philadelphia PA 19147	Daryaganj
United Kingdom	USA	New Delhi 110002
www.koganpage.com		India

© John Adair, 2010

The right of John Adair to be identified as the author of this work has been asserted by him in accordance with the Copyright, Designs and Patents Act 1988.

ISBN   978 0 7494 6203 1
E-ISBN   978 0 7494 6204 8

British Library Cataloguing-in-Publication Data

A CIP record for this book is available from the British Library.

Library of Congress Cataloging-in-Publication Data

Adair, John Eric, 1934–
    Strategic leadership : how to think and plan strategically and provide direction / John Adair. – 1st ed.
        p. cm.
    ISBN 978-0-7494-6203-1 – ISBN 978-0-7494-6204-8   1. Leadership.   2. Strategy.
I. Title.
    HD57.7.A2756 2010
    658.4'092–dc22

                                                                                      2010017895

Typeset by Graphicraft Ltd, Hong Kong
Printed and bound in India by Replika Press Pvt Ltd

CONTENTS

LIST OF FIGURES

LIST OF TABLES

ABOUT THE AUTHOR

John Adair is now widely regarded as the world's leading authority on leadership and leadership development. The author of 30 books on the subject, he has been named as one of the 40 people worldwide who have contributed most to the development of management thought and practice.

Educated at St Paul's School, John Adair has enjoyed a varied and colourful career. He served as adjutant in a Bedouin regiment in the Arab Legion, worked as a deckhand on an Arctic trawler and had a spell as an orderly in a hospital operating theatre. After Cambridge he became Senior Lecturer in Military History and Leadership Training Adviser at the Royal Military Academy, Sandhurst, before becoming the first Director of Studies at St George's House in Windsor Castle and then Associate Director of the Industrial Society. Later he became the world's first Professor in Leadership Studies at the University of Surrey. He also helped to found Europe's first Centre for Leadership Studies at the University of Exeter.

John Adair is currently the United Nations Chair of Strategic Leadership based on the United Nations Staff College in Turin. His recent books, published by Kogan Page, include *Not Bosses But Leaders*, *The Inspirational Leader* and *How to Grow Leaders*.

INTRODUCTION

Those having torches will pass them on to others.
Plato (429–347 BC)

Welcome to this book. I hope you will find here a clear introduction to your role as a strategic leader – what you are being paid to do. The emphasis of the book is not on a methodology. Its focus is on encouraging you to ask the right questions; to look beyond what you think you know; to focus on tomorrow rather than yesterday.

A strategic leader is essentially the leader of an organization. An *effective* strategic leader is one who delivers the goods in terms of what an organization naturally expects from its leadership in times of change.

As you will have gathered by now, this book is written primarily for those who are about to become strategic leaders or who aspire to be in that role. You may, of course, already be head of an organization, or know that you are next in line for such a role, or you may simply be aware that the path of your vocation is leading you in that direction.

That doesn't exhaust the list of those who can read this book with profit. In large organizations there is – or should be – a strategic leadership team working under the conductor's baton of the head person. Obviously the more each member knows of the principles and practice of strategic leadership the better they can support and complement the contribution of their leader.

Do not assume, however, that this book only applies to those who work in large or medium-sized organizations. The body of knowledge and ideas it contains, especially the parts relating to strategic thinking, is equally relevant to those in charge of small organizations, and indeed to those like myself who work in unstructured fields. As the Roman playwright Plautus said, '*Ergomet sum mihi imperator*' – 'I am myself my own commander.' Today each of us has to be our own strategic leader.

Leading the way – whether for an organization or for yourself – is never easy. I hope that this book equips you for the challenge and that you enjoy reading it too.

The book is largely self-explanatory. Part One maps and explores the sources and fundamentals of the role of strategic leadership. Part Two moves on to what you have to do today to be effective in the role, focusing on the seven generic functions that make up the role of a strategic leader.

The summary of key points at the end of each chapter is designed as a concise aide-mémoire for revision purposes, but occasionally I throw in a new idea just to see if you are still awake! I have included some exercises – for this book is essentially practical – and I suggest that you ask yourself questions as you go along in order to relate what I am saying to your own situation. The more that you put into the reading of the book, the more you will get the best out of it.

To get the most out of a book like this one, however, you do need *a wide span of relevance*. By that I mean that we naturally look for examples or case studies in our own field, such as business or education, and think that these ones only are relevant to our situation. But you should be able to see relevance to your situation in the examples of, say, an orchestral conductor or a Greek general. It is the same principle, incidentally, that lies behind creative thinking: the sparks of meaning jump between two or more apparently unconnected things to produce new ideas. It is also fun to think like this.

For there is an underlying unity in strategic leadership, whatever field you are in and however structured or unstructured your work in it may be. Walter Bagehot, a 19th-century banker, economist and journalist famous for his insights into economics and political questions, understood this well:

> The summits of the various kinds of business are, like the tops of mountains, much more alike than the parts below – the bare principles are much the same; it is only the rich variegated details of the lower strata that so contrast with one another.
>
> But it needs travelling to know that the summits are the same. Those who live on one mountain believe that their mountain is wholly unlike all others.

When you continue your observation of effective strategic leaders in organizations, encouraged I hope by these pages, you will be increasingly aware of how much they have in common. Therefore you can draw lessons and insights from many sources in order to grow as a strategic leader. And something of the spirit of leadership which is in the best of them – the torches they bear – will light a torch in your spirit that will burn for the rest of your life.

> There are many paths to the top of the mountain
> But the view is always the same.
>
> *Chinese proverb*

PART ONE

THE ROLE

01

STRATEGIC LEADERSHIP

Dux erat ille ducum *(He was leader of leaders)*.
Ovid (43 BC–17/18 AD), Heroides

Peter Drucker is widely regarded as one of the most original thinkers on management; indeed he pretty much invented the subject. He wrote 38 books over six decades; he covered a lot of ground! He focused on getting managers to ask the right questions; to look beyond what they thought they knew; to focus on tomorrow rather than yesterday. If anything this mindset is now more valuable in the digital age than it was in the industrial age.

Some years ago, when I was first thinking of writing a book on strategic leadership, I was invited to co-lead a seminar for senior bankers with Peter Drucker. Over lunch I had the opportunity of seeking his advice on the project I had in mind – it was rather like getting a personal tutorial from the creator of modern management.

'Do you know when managers began to talk about strategy?' Peter Drucker asked me during the course of our discussion about strategic leadership.

'I imagine it was sometime ... no, I really don't know,' I replied. 'When was it?'

'In 1964 I submitted a book to my American publisher,' he said, 'which I had called *Management Strategy*. They insisted that I should change the title, as "strategy" was a military term and business-executive readers would either not understand it or perceive it as irrelevant. So it appeared as *Management for Results*.'

'Where did the idea come from to bring in the concept in the first place?' I asked.

'I believe it stemmed from Robert McNamara in the Kennedy era,' Drucker replied. 'McNamara moved between heading up the Pentagon as Secretary of Defense to being President of the Ford Motor Company.'

In fact, one or two books did appear about that time which used the word *strategy* in the business context, notably Alfred Chandler's *Strategy and Structure: Chapters in the History of American Enterprise* (1962) and Igor Ansoff's *Corporate Strategy* (1965). But, as far as I know, I was the first to introduce the phrase 'strategic leadership' in the early 1970s and it is now in wide use.

MILITARY ORIGINS OF STRATEGIC LEADERSHIP

Originally, strategy (*strategia* in Greek) meant strategic leadership – the art of being a commander-in-chief.

Strategy is in fact made up of two ancient Greek words. The first part comes from *stratos*, which means an army spread out as in camp, and thus a large body of people. The second part, *–egy*, comes from the Greek verb 'to lead'. There is a rough breathing mark in the Greek, giving an *h* sound, which explains the spelling of the English word *hegemony* – meaning the leadership of one nation over others – which is derived from it.

It was Athens, rivalled only by Sparta, which claimed the hegemony of the Greek city states. Around 500 BC a senior commander in the Athenian army came to be called a *strategos*, leader of the army. The English word we use to translate this word is *general*. It literally means something (or someone) that is applicable to the whole. So a military general is the person who is accountable for the whole army as well as its parts.

In the Athenian citizen army during the fifth century BC, there were 10 large units based on the old tribal networks in the city. Later in Athenian history these units were commanded by what we would call professional soldiers, but in the early days the 10 *strategoi* were elected by their fellow citizens. To be elected a *strategos* was an important step on the political ladder for any ambitious young Athenian. Great leaders of the city state, such as Thermistocles and Pericles, had risen by this very route. But the need for election acted as a hurdle: how could you get your fellow citizens – the voters – to vote in your favour? One man seems to have thought about this question – Socrates.

The son of a stonemason, Socrates constantly drew the analogy between the skills of artisans and craftsmen – the physician, the leather seller, the metal worker – and the wider roles and responsibilities of a citizen's life, indeed that very life itself. All these practical skills can be learned by careful analysis, education and training and, where necessary, by experience, as everyone agreed. Socrates always professed himself unable to understand why the higher or more difficult arts – political leadership, statesmanship, the administration of justice – are not acknowledged to be susceptible of the same treatment.

Socrates himself wrote no books. Our principal sources of information about him are the writings of two of his inner circle: Plato and Xenophon. As they both wrote their various works in the form of Socratic dialogues it is not easy to determine whether the voice we hear is that of Socrates or those of Plato and Xenophon.

Encouraging others by confessing his own lack of knowledge, Socrates set out to think things through for himself in discussion. Thereby he led his interlocutors on a journey of the mind. Towards the end of it they began to see and discover for themselves what knowledge or skill is required in any human being.

Socrates believed that the good life is about knowing the good and knowing how to seek it in any circumstances. For Plato that journey would lead him ever further away from the practical issues of living and working that interested Socrates, far into the realm of abstract ideas, the domain of philosophy which would for ever bear his stamp. But his fellow student, Xenophon, would take a very different course. For, at the age of 26, Xenophon would become the commander-in-chief of a Greek army.

One day, Xenophon tells us, Socrates engaged in discussion with a newly elected cavalry commander. As Xenophon himself was elected to that office it is tempting to believe that this is a piece of autobiography and he is describing here his first encounter with 'The Thinker'.

Under questioning from Socrates, the young man agreed that his seeking of the rank of commander could not have been because he wanted to be the first in the cavalry charge, for, as Socrates pointed out, the mounted archers usually rode ahead of the commander into battle. Nor could it have been simply in order to get himself known by everyone – even madmen, he conceded, could achieve that. He accepted Socrates's suggestion that it must have been because he wanted to leave the Athenian cavalry in better condition than when he found it.

Xenophon, later both a renowned authority on horsemanship and author of a textbook on commanding cavalry, had no difficulty in explaining what needs to be done to achieve that end. The young commander, for example, must improve the quality of the cavalry mounts; he must school new recruits – both horses and men – in equestrian skills and then teach the troopers their cavalry tactics. All these points emerged step by step out of the dialogue.

'And have you considered how to make the men obey you?' continued Socrates. 'Because without that, horses and men, however good and gallant, are of no use.'

'True, but what is the best way of encouraging them to obey, Socrates?' asked the young man.

'Well, I suppose you know that under all conditions human beings are most willing to obey those whom they believe to be the best. Thus in sickness they most readily obey the doctor, on board ship the pilot, on a farm the farmer, whom they think to be the most skilled in his business.'

'Yes, certainly,' said his student.

'Then it is likely that in horsemanship too, one who clearly knows best what ought to be done will most easily gain the obedience of the others.'

Xenophon captures here a very distinct theme in Socrates's teaching on leadership. In harmony with the rest of his doctrine (for, despite his pose of ignorance, Socrates had ideas of his own), it emphasizes the importance of *knowledge* in leadership. People will obey willingly only those whom they perceive to be better qualified or more knowledgeable than themselves in a particular field.

LEARNING GENERALSHIP

Although neither ancient Athens nor any of the other Greek cities had anything resembling what we would call a business school, the figure of the itinerant teacher or guru speaking to audiences for fat fees on such subjects as the art of public speaking, generalship or how to be happy and successful was a familiar one. These sophists, as they were called, were clever men, some more so than others, known for their adroit, subtle, plausible reasoning but lacking in substance. Socrates and other philosophers regarded them as glib, superficial and out for money (Socrates himself did not charge fees).

Socrates once met a young man who had attended a seminar on strategic leadership (or generalship) conducted for money by one of these business gurus – a man called Dionysodurus. Socrates professed himself to be shocked at the instruction his young friend had received.

'Tell us the first lesson in generalship Dionysodurus gave you,' asked Socrates.

'The first was like the last,' the young man replied. 'He taught me tactics – nothing else.'

'But that is only a small part of generalship,' replied Socrates. By question and answer he then led the young man into a much fuller understanding of the knowledge and abilities required for a successful military leader. A general, for example, must be good at administration, so that the army is properly supplied with military equipment and provisions.

Moreover, as Xenophon knew from his own experience, a general should ideally possess a number of personal qualities and skills:

> He must be resourceful, active, careful, hard and quick-witted; he must be both gentle and brutal, at once straight-forward and designing, capable of both caution and surprise, lavish and rapacious, generous and mean, skilful in defence and attack, and there are many other qualifications, some natural, some acquired, that are necessary to one as a general.

Even on the all-important subject of tactics, Socrates found the instruction given to his young friend by Dionysodurus to be deficient. Did Dionysodurus give no advice on where and how to use each formation? Was no guidance given on when to modify deployments and tactics according to the needs of the many different kinds of situations one encounters in war? The young man insisted that this was the case.

'Then you must go back and ask for your money back,' said Socrates. 'For if Dionysodurus knows the answer to these questions and has a conscience, he will be ashamed to send you home ill-taught.'

The point is that Dionysodurus had an extremely limited concept of what strategy was all about. He saw it as being little more than battlefield tactics – how to handle one's army when it was face to face with the enemy. And even he taught that as a rigid methodology: a series of set-piece manoeuvres or drills. He evidently taught as if from a textbook, but he lacked military experience. So he would not have been able to answer any questions, such as when to use a particular tactic rather than another. In other words, he was not teaching people the art of generalship.

There is a parallel to this blinkered view of strategic leader-ship in our own day. If you pick up any book with strategy in its title, you will almost certainly find that it is about marketing strategy for commercial business in the narrowest sense of the word 'business'. Ask for your money back!

THE ART OF THE COMMANDER-IN-CHIEF

In contrast to sophists like Dionysodurus, Socrates – who did have some military experience – saw clearly that strategy – *strategia* – is *the art of being a commander-in-chief*. And that art encompasses far more than battlefield tactics. Notably, it is about the *soldiers* – their training, their spirit, their morale and their will to fight. The highest level of military command is a role, in other words, that calls for *leadership*.

Napoleon and Wellington famously had their differences on the battlefields of Europe, but one thing they agreed upon: the greatest general of all time was Hannibal, the leader of the Carthaginian army in its great struggle against Rome.

Carthage, of course, lost the war and Hannibal went into exile far from the ruins of Carthage in order to evade the assassins hired by Rome to kill him. Antiochus, a Greek king in Syria, offered Hannibal a refuge. One day he invited Hannibal to accompany him to hear a travelling Greek sophist lecturing on the subject of generalship. Doubtless Hannibal could not have got out of attending without offending his host.

'Well, what did you think of it?' Antiochus inquired eagerly at the end.

Hannibal looked at the king with his one remaining eye and thought for a moment. 'In my time I have had to listen to some old fools,' he replied, 'but this one beats them all!'

TRANSFERABLE SKILLS

Socrates (or Xenophon) was the first person in the world to see that the role of being a *strategos* – a strategic leader – is essentially the same whatever kind of organization you happen to lead. Therefore, at least in theory, the constituent *functions* that make up that role are transferable from one field to another. The Greeks had minds that were both abstract and analytical (another Greek word by origin), so – as we shall see in a moment – they began the work that I have been destined to continue – namely to analyse the (abstract) generic role of strategic leader into its constituent parts.

Notice, however, that this latter insight seems to cut across the grain of the Socratic teaching that we have established already, namely that authority belongs to the expert or the specialist, the one who is technically or professionally master of their field. The issue emerges clearly in a conversation that Socrates – according to Xenophon – once had with a soldier called Nicomachides.

Once, on seeing Nicomachides returning from the elections, Socrates asked him, 'Who have been chosen generals, Nicomachides?'

'Isn't it just like the Athenians?' Nicomachides replied. 'They have not chosen me after all the hard work I have done since I was called up, in the command of company or regiment, though I have been so often wounded in action.' Here he uncovered and showed his scars. 'They have chosen Antisthenes, who has never served in a marching regiment nor distinguished himself in the cavalry and understands nothing but money making.'

'Isn't that a recommendation?' said Socrates. 'Supposing he proves capable of supplying the men's needs?'

'Why,' retorted Nicomachides, 'merchants also are capable of making money, but that doesn't make them fit to command an army!'

'But,' replied Socrates, 'Antisthenes also is eager for victory, and that is a good point in a general. Whenever he has been choir master, you know, his choir has always won.'

'No doubt,' conceded Nicomachides, 'but there is no analogy between the handling of a choir and of an army.'

'But you see,' said Socrates, 'though Antisthenes knows nothing about music or choir training, he showed himself capable of finding the best experts in these activities. And therefore if he finds and prefers the best men in warfare as in choir training, it is likely that he will be victorious in that too; and probably he will be more ready to spend money on winning a battle with the whole state than on winning a choral competition with his tribe.'

'Do you mean to say, Socrates, that the man who succeeds with a chorus will also succeed with an army?'

'I mean that, whatever a man directs, if he knows what he wants and can get it he will be a good director, whether he directs a chorus, an estate, a city or an army.'

'Really, Socrates,' cried Nicomachides, 'I should never have thought to hear you say that a good businessman would make a good general!'

By his familiar method of patient cross-examination, Socrates then proceeded to secure agreement from Nicomachides that successful businessmen and generals perform much the same functions. Then Socrates proceeded to identify six of these functions or skills:

- Selecting the right person for the job;

- Punishing the bad and rewarding the good;

- Winning the goodwill of those under them;

- Attracting allies and helpers;

- Keeping what they have gained;

- Being strenuous and industrious in their own work.

'All these are common to both,' Nicomachides eventually agreed, but added, 'but fighting is not.'

'But surely both are bound to find enemies?' said Socrates.

'Oh yes, they are.'

'Then is it not important for both to get the better of them?'

'Undoubtedly, but you don't say how business capacity will help when it comes to fighting.'

'That is just where it will be most helpful,' Socrates concluded. 'For the good businessman, through his knowledge that nothing profits or pays like a victory in the field, and nothing is so utterly unprofitable and entails such heavy loss as a defeat, will be eager to seek and avoid what leads to defeat, will be prompt to engage the enemy if he sees he is strong enough to win, and, above all, will avoid an engagement when he is not ready.'

THE ART OF INSPIRING OTHERS

For Xenophon the third function – winning the goodwill of those under them – was an absolutely vital function of a commander-in-chief. In his own long military experience he had seen on so many occasions what a difference it makes. *Strategia* without leadership is not *strategia* as the Greeks understood it. In a book on the management of estates, Xenophon wrote:

> For some make their men unwilling to work and to take risks, disinclined and unwilling to obey, except under compulsion, and actually proud of defying their commander: yes, and they cause them to have no sense of dishonour when something disgraceful occurs.
>
> Contrast the genius, the brave and skilful leader: let him take over the command of these same troops, or of others if you like. What effect has he on them? They are ashamed to do a disgraceful act, think it better to obey, and take a pride in obedience, working cheerfully, every man and all together, when it is necessary to work.
>
> Just as a love of work may spring up in the mind of a private soldier here and here, so a whole army under the influence of a good leader is inspired by love of work and ambition to distinguish itself under the commander's eye. Let this be the feeling of the rank and file for their commander, then he is the best leader – it is not a matter of being the best with bow and javelin, nor riding the best horse and being foremost in danger, nor being the perfect mounted warrior, but of being able to make his soldiers feel that they must follow him through fire and in any adventure.
>
> So, too, in private industries, the man in authority – supervisor or manager – who can make the workers keen, industrious and persevering – he is the man who gives a lift to the business and swells the profits.

For Xenophon, this kind of leadership is quite simply 'the greatest thing in every operation that makes any demand on the labour of men'.

If leaders are made in the sense that they can acquire the authority of knowledge, are they born as far as the capacity to inspire is concerned? It is tempting to conclude that this is the case. The ability to give people the intellectual and moral strength to venture or persevere in the presence of danger, fear or difficulty is not the common endowment of all men and women. Xenophon, however, did believe that at least the basic principles of it could be acquired through education, as he had experienced himself with Socrates.

'Mind you, I do not go as far as to say that this can be learnt at sight or at a single hearing,' he wrote in the conclusion of *Oeconomicus*. 'On the contrary, to acquire these powers a man needs education.' Natural potential is most important, he continues. But in some men leadership amounts to a gift, something akin to genius that suggests something more of divine origin than human.

This 'power to win willing obedience' may seem ultimately as if it is a gift of the gods, writes Xenophon, but it is not capriciously bestowed. The true beneficiaries of it are 'those who devote themselves to seeking wisdom'. There speaks the voice of Socrates!

This chapter has been devoted to the world's first thoughts – in the person of Xenophon – on strategic leadership. He saw it as a transferable art or skill, and identified its essential principles for the first time. Although nature equipped some men and women for leadership more than others – some even having a gift amounting to genius for it – everyone can develop their natural ability for leading people. Like Xenophon you have to learn to think for yourself about the role of strategic leader and how to apply its constituent functions in your own field of work.

KEY POINTS

■ Strategy as a word is a fairly recent borrowing from military vocabulary. It reflects its more modern military usage – strategy as opposed to tactics.

▓ In fact, this modern idea of strategy is far too narrow. Strategy or *strategia*, properly understood, is the leadership of a large body of people, such as a *stratos* – an army spread out.

▓ As armies were the largest work-related organizations for some 3,000 years before the rise of big business in the 19th century, it is not surprising that the concept of strategic leadership developed into its first full-blown form in the role of a commander-in-chief.

▓ The contemporary tendency to equate strategic leadership with formulating strategy reflects a basic misunderstanding of the concept. If you look closely at great generals, strategy in the narrow sense occupies only a small amount of their time.

▓ *Strategia*, the art of being a commander-in-chief, includes good administration, good communications, the training and equipping of the soldiers under one's command.

▓ Most of the functions and qualities of strategic leadership are transferable from one field to another. They include: selecting, punishing and rewarding, building alliances, and being hard-working.

▓ Some qualifications of a strategic leader are natural and some are acquired. Chief among them is the ability to win the goodwill of those under them.

There is small risk a leader will be regarded with contempt by those he leads if, whatever he may have to ask others to do, he shows himself best able to perform.

Xenophon

02

THE GENERIC ROLE OF LEADER

Truth is the daughter of search.   **Arab proverb**

What is leadership? I first asked myself this question when I was just 18 and coming to the end of my schooldays at St Paul's School in London. I had chosen to give a lecture on the subject of 'Leadership in History' to the school historical society, which I had founded. Someone present wrote this brief summary of my talk for the school magazine.

> Leadership, he said, could be defined as the activity of influencing people to pursue a certain course; there must also be some power of mind behind the leader.

> Leadership is not merely the authority of the commander, but contains by necessity some strange strength of personality which attracts the ordinary man. It is only when the times are favourable that a man of destiny can come into his own.

Although leadership may change in this aspect from age to age, the qualities of a leader are the same.

Many years later, having devoted much of my professional life to leadership and leadership development, I find that this summary is not far off the mark in reflecting what I think today. Sometimes first thoughts are best.

Incidentally, I reckon that identifying the right questions to ask in any subject is like finding a golden key, the key that unlocks the door of the corridor that leads to knowledge. In the course of time my simple boyhood question evolved into the form today in which I ask myself – and you:

Why is it that one person rather than others is perceived to be – or accepted as – a leader in a work group?

There has been a long quest – dating back over a hundred years – to find a satisfactory answer to this key question. The real breakthrough, however, occurred in the middle of the last century when we discovered the generic role of leader. It evolved from the empirical study of working groups.

GROUP NEEDS

Working groups are wholes that are more than the sum of their parts. Groups are always unique – they have a 'group personality', so that, for example, what works in one group may not work in another. But, different as they are (like individual persons), working groups share certain things in common: needs. These are:

▪ The need to accomplish the common task. Why is an organization formed? To achieve a task which an individual or small group cannot do on its own.

▪ The need to be held together and maintained as a working unity – a whole and not just a collection of discordant parts.

▓ The need that individuals bring with them into any organization.

THE THREE CIRCLES MODEL

These three areas of need are dynamic and interactive, and they are depicted as such in my model shown in Figure 2.1. As the Chinese proverb says, a picture is worth a thousand words.

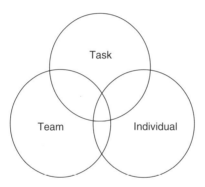

Figure 2.1 *The three circles model: the interaction of areas of need*

To explore, for example, the negative interactions, place a coin over the Task circle in Figure 2.1. It will immediately cover segments of the other two circles as well. In other words, lack of a task – or failure to achieve it – will affect both team maintenance, for example by increasing disruptive tendencies, and also the area of individual needs, very possibly by lowering member satisfaction within the group. Move the coin on to the Team circle, and again the impact of a near-complete lack of relationships in the group on both task and individual needs may be seen at a glance. Cover the Individual circle – imagine an individual who feels frustrated in terms of their needs and consequently tends to withdraw psychologically from engagement with the Task or Team.

These three interlocking circles therefore illustrate the general point that each area of need exerts an influence upon the other two; they are not watertight compartments.

NECESSARY FUNCTIONS

In order to meet the three areas of need, as we have seen, certain functions have to be performed. A function may be defined as the proper or characteristic action of a person or thing. It is often one of a group of related actions, each contributing to a large action. For example, I write with a pen and in writing this sentence, both hand and eyes are fulfilling their normal and characteristic functions to contribute to a single activity. In the context of the larger activity of leading, such functions as *defining the task* and *planning* are clearly required.

Assemble a group of children in the playground with a task to perform, with or without appointing a leader, and you should be able to observe some of these functions being performed – or not performed, as the case may be.

THE GENERIC ROLE OF A LEADER

So far we have agreed only that there are *three overlapping areas of need* present in all working groups, and that in order to meet them certain key *functions* have to be performed. The next step is the idea that these functions hang together in a set: together they form the core of *the generic role of leader*. The discovery of this generic role crowned a quest by thinkers that began long ago in ancient Athens and China, and was pursued intently in recent times.

The generic role of leader – the essential requirements of a leader – is simple. The core role at any level refracts into broad functions derived from the three circles model. The three general functions are shown in Figure 2.2.

Achieving the common task

Building and maintaining the team

Motivating and developing the individual

Figure 2.2 *The three circles model: the broad functions of strategic leadership*

The generic role can then be broken down further into more specific functions, such as *planning* and *evaluating*. But you should notice that these functions – and the others explored in Part Two – are not assignable to any one circle: they have effects for good or bad on all three.

For example, 'planning' looks on the surface like a task function. But there is nothing like a bad plan to disintegrate a team, lower morale and frustrate individuals. Planning hits all three circles: the model is a unity, or, more accurately, a diversity in unity.

Teams that come together to pursue a self-chosen task, such as trade unions or sports clubs, tend to *elect* their own leaders, who are responsible ultimately to the team. Where tasks are given to the team, on the other hand, the leader tends to be *appointed* by higher authority and sent to it as part of the package deal. In this case the leader is accountable first to the appointing authority and only secondly – if at all – to the team. The leader is responsible for all three circles.

There is a set of common functions – things you have to do or get others to do – if these three overlapping areas of responsibility are to be met. They are summarized in Table 2.1.

Table 2.1   Leadership functions

Defining the task	What are the purpose, aims and objectives? Why is this work worthwhile?
Planning	A plan answers the question of *how* you are going to get from where you are now to where you want to be. There is nothing like a bad plan to break up a group or frustrate individuals.
Briefing	The ability to communicate, to get across to people the task and the plan.
Controlling	Making sure that all resources and energies are properly harnessed.
Supporting	Setting and maintaining organizational and team values and standards.
Informing	Bringing information to the group and from the group – the *linking* function of leadership.
Reviewing	Establishing and applying the success criteria appropriate to the field.

These are best called *leadership functions*. Together they constitute the role of a leader, but always remember that leadership is more than the sum of those parts. You need to invest in it your heart and mind and spirit.

If you exercise the art of leadership properly, you will generate a *sense of responsibility* in the team as a whole, so that members naturally want to respond to the three sets of need. But as the appointed or elected leader, make no mistake that it is you who are *accountable* at the end of the day. It is the leader who should expect to be dismissed or resign if the task is not achieved, or the team disintegrates into warring factions, or the individuals lapse into sullen apathy. That is why leaders usually get paid more than the team members. Are you ready for that?

REALITIES OF COMMAND

Almost everybody thought that it was the French general Marshal Joffre who had won the battle of the Marne in the opening year of the First World War – the crucial battle that had stemmed the advance of the German army in front of Paris – but some refused to agree. One day a newspaper man appealed to Joffre: 'Will you tell me who did win the battle of the Marne?' 'I can't answer that,' said the Marshal. 'But I can tell you that if the battle of the Marne had been lost the blame would have been on me.'

A LEADER'S QUALIFICATIONS

As Xenophon said, some of these are natural and some are acquired. The natural qualities that are expected in a person occupying the generic role of leader in any field can be developed by study and experiences.

There is still room for debate on what these personal qualities are. My own view is that a leader should, first and foremost, possess and exemplify the qualities expected or required in their field. So a military leader, for example, will need physical courage as well as the other characteristics of any good soldier. But there are some more generic leadership qualities, such as *enthusiasm*, *integrity* – the quality that makes people trust you – the combination of *toughness* or demandingness and *fairness*, *warmth* or *humanity, energy* or *resilience* and *humility* – by which I mean lack of arrogance.

HUMILITY IN ACTION

'A sense of humility is a quality I have observed in every leader whom I have deeply admired,' wrote Eisenhower. 'I have seen Winston Churchill with humble tears of gratitude on his cheeks as he thanked people for their help to Britain and the Allied cause.' He continued: 'My own conviction is that every leader should have enough humility to accept, publicly, the responsibility for the mistakes of the subordinates he has himself selected, and likewise to give them credit, publicly, for their triumphs. I am aware that some popular theories of leadership hold that the top man must always keep his 'image' bright and shining. I believe, however, that in the long run fairness and honesty, and a generous attitude towards subordinates and associates, pay off.'

In a memorial speech on Eisenhower delivered to Congress in 1969, the President of the United States cited as the key to Eisenhower's character an undelivered statement prepared for broadcast over the radio in the event of the D-Day landings ending in disaster. It read as follows:

'Our landings in the Cherbourg–Havre area have failed to gain a satisfactory foothold and I have withdrawn the troops. My decision to attack at this time and place was based upon the best information available. The troops, the air force and navy, did all that bravery and devotion to duty could do. If any blame or fault attaches to the attempt it is mine alone.'

This list is not exhaustive, for with leadership there are always facets of the diamond that catch the light in some individuals in certain circumstances and not in others. So you can always study the qualities of leaders and see – or see afresh – new facets. *Humour*, for example, not mentioned above, can be a powerful leadership quality.

No one has the sum of all these contributory qualities, for the ideal leader is a concept, not a person. We are all like magpies, mixtures of strengths and weaknesses. But you should aim to develop the natural qualities you have that fall within the general flight path indicated above. If you try and fail, the good news is that you will tend to become more humble; and humility, as I have already hinted, is the most useful leadership quality as well!

THE INTELLECTUAL SIDE OF LEADERSHIP

The personal qualities I have mentioned so far can be classified roughly as characteristics or tendencies in your personality, temperament or character. But since the days of Socrates, the importance of a leader's *technical or professional knowledge* – relative to the other members of the group – has been rightly emphasized.

Apart from the authority that stems from being appointed or elected to be leader, apart from any personal charm, it is possessing the kind of technical or professional knowledge which commands respect in your field that will confer authority upon you. Authority flows to the one who knows.

The knowledge that a leader needs or acquires today is more than technical expertise. It is essential to understand the generic role of leader and the constituent functions, and to be trained in using them. But only you can apply that knowledge in your given field, and in all the myriad changing acts and scenes of the drama which is your vocational life. And that calls for *practical intelligence*.

For knowing what to do in situations is partly a factor of technical/professional knowledge and partly a factor of knowledge about people (if those situations involve people, as in the case of leadership they invariably will). Here two other factors – *intelligence* and *experience* – come into the equation. In the Socratic concept of *knowledge*, you could say that intelligence and experience are inbuilt. That may be so, but it is worth artificially separating them out here for the sake of understanding.

As a general common-sense principle, a leader should be of at least average intelligence. As Ordway Tead wrote long ago in America's best book on leadership, *The Art of Leadership* (1935): 'What little scientific evidence there is above the consensus of observable facts seems to point to the truth that, other qualities being equal, the person of greater intelligence will probably make the better leader.'

Intelligence is the faculty of understanding. Mental alertness, problem-solving ability and keen perception of relationships are all implicit in intelligence. Mental ability in this wider and more informal sense is obviously more transferable than any specific technical know-how. 'The few studies available,' continues Tead, 'indicate also that this higher intelligence factor in leaders correlates with *versatility*. The tentative conclusion seems to be that those capable of leading in one field are likely to be found potentially high in capacity to lead in several fields. The kind of eager, alert, outreaching mental quality which marks the leader predisposes him to use his powers in several directions.'

Intelligence in this context includes the ability:

▓ to see the point;
▓ to sense relationships and analogies quickly;
▓ to identify the essentials in a complex picture;

- to 'put two and two together';
- to find the salient factors in past experience which are helpful in shedding light on present difficulties;
- to be able to distinguish clearly between ends and means;
- to appraise situations readily;
- to see their significance in the total setting of present and past experience;
- to get the cue as to the likely line of wise action.

These overlap considerably, but taken together they offer an idea of the kind of practical intelligence or sense we are talking about.

In the list above, the interdependence of intelligence with experience is evident. Experience can be either experience of life in general, which tends to come with age, or relevant professional experience in a given situation. Familiarity is based upon considerable actual practice. You have personally encountered, undergone or lived through situations not unlike the one now faced.

By implication, this past immersion in a subject or field has resulted in superior understanding. Sometimes, however, what is called experience yields no gain in wisdom; for some – the non-learners – it means no more than a piling-up of involvements. Marshal Saxe's donkey, it is said, went on 20 campaigns carrying his master's baggage, but learned nothing about the art of war.

The Greeks had a word for this combination of intelligence and experience in practical affairs: *phronesis*. It was translated into Latin as *prudentia* and thence into English as *prudence*. Essentially, prudence suggests action that is the outcome of wisdom gained by experience. The ability to govern and discipline oneself by the use of reason, sagacity or shrewdness in the management of affairs, prudence is the use of resources, caution or circumspection as to danger or risk – you can see why Aristotle placed *phronesis* among the 'intellectual virtues'. As prudence carries a slight overtone of restraint, a better translation of *phronesis* in English today is practical wisdom.

KEY POINTS

▦ A leader should personify the qualities expected in any worker in their field, as well as some of the more generic attributes of a leader – for instance, enthusiasm, integrity, toughness and fairness, humanity, energy and resilience.

▦ The generic role of any leader can be defined by the model of the three circles – task, team and individual – and then broken down further – especially for selection or training purposes – into functions.

▦ Which circle is dominant in the mind of a leader at any one time depends upon the circumstances. The model is dynamic and not static. It does suggest, however, the need for a balance over the longer term.

▦ The generic role of leader, as discovered in this chapter, has withstood the test of time as no other theory or model in the field has done. It is now taken universally to be true. As Albert Einstein wrote:

Ethical axioms are found and tested not very differently from the axioms of science. Truth is what stands the test of experience.

Out of My Later Years (1950)

03

LEVELS OF LEADERSHIP

An army of a thousand is easy to find, but how difficult to find a general.   **Chinese proverb**

Leadership is discernible on three broad levels: team, operational and strategic. These constitute the natural hierarchy in all working organizations, although the levels overlap and may be subdivided in a variety of ways. Fortunately the same generic role of leader applies at all levels. What changes with level, of course, is the *complexity* factor – complexity, incidentally in all three circles, as the environment is constantly changing. An *organization* is very different from a small *work group*.

UNDERSTANDING ORGANIZATION

To organize means arranging so that the whole aggregate works as a unit, with each element having a proper function.

The Greek *organon* meant literally 'that with which one works' and is related to *ergon*, work. It meant a tool or instrument, especially a musical instrument or a surgical instrument. But it was also used figuratively of the parts of the human body that were regarded as instruments of sense of faculty.

That sense of something made deliberately for man's use carries over into our concept of an organization. The *–ation* at the end of these long Latin- and Greek-derived words means the action or process itself or the resulting condition. So an organization is what you get as a result of organizing, which in turn means systematic arranging for a definite purpose.

There is a useful distinction to be made between an *organization* and a *community*, though both are the products of humans imposing order on chaos. A community derives from the family, kindred group or tribe and has order through acceptance of common law and a form of government. Our nation states stand in this line of descent. Organizations, by contrast, are hunting parties at large. They are formed and developed with a particular form of work or – in the most general sense – task in mind.

You can eat apples, pears, grapes or bananas, but you cannot eat fruit. For fruit is a generic and therefore abstract concept. In a similar vein, you can see and experience life in organizations such as an army, church, government department, bank or computer company, but you will never encounter organization as such, apart from its forms. You cannot see or touch it. It is an abstract concept too, like fruit.

Why bother with such an abstract concept? Because the world of organizations is extremely complex. They differ in size and shape, in purpose or function. Some are young and thrusting, others are old and venerable institutions. Not only does national culture colour them, but they develop their own organizational cultures.

Faced with this bewildering variety, it is natural for the human mind to search for what is generic and common. It is a seeking of simplicity in the face of apparent complexity, but not for a purely academic end. For the concept of strategic leadership as at least theoretically a transferable art depends upon organizations having – beneath the surface – a generic unity. So organization is worth exploring further.

The only way we can think about something as abstract as organizations is by analogy or metaphor. One of the oldest metaphors used to help us understand is the human body. An organization – any organization – is a form of a whole made up of interdependent parts. Those two aspects – whole and parts – are generic; they are the essence of organization. The human-body metaphor gives us some of our generic language about organization, such as *head* or *chief, corporate* and *member*.

If we widen the metaphor and think of the human person and not just the body, that suggests two ideas. First, just as we are all unique and have our own distinctive personality, so groups – if they stay together – develop a *group personality*. And organizations, which are teams writ large, also form an *organizational personality*, or corporate culture as it is commonly called. It finds expression in the behaviour typical in that group or organization. Remember, therefore, that every organization you encounter is unique, and one of your first requirements as its strategic leader will be to be aware of that uniqueness.

Different though we all are as individual persons, however, we share some things in common, such as the attribute of personality itself. Most obviously, we all have needs – for food, drink and shelter, for example. Following that analogy, all organizations have three areas of need present in them.

Clearly we are back now to the three circles model – the great discovery that the three areas of need in any organization will act upon each other in an inter-influential way for good or ill.

Therefore the role of a strategic leader is to do for the whole what other leaders should accomplish for the parts.

DIFFERENT LEADERSHIP RESPONSIBILITIES

Leadership exists on different levels. Thinking of organizations, there are three broad levels or domains of leadership, as shown in Figure 3.1 and Table 3.1.

The need is for excellence at all three levels of leadership. The secret to business success lies in teamwork between and within each of these levels.

Figure 3.1   *Levels of leadership*

Table 3.1   Levels of leadership

Strategic	The leader of a whole organization, with a number of operational leaders under their personal direction.
Operational	The leader of one of the main parts of the organization, with more than one team leader under their control. It is already a case of being a leader of leaders.
Team	The leader of a team of up to 20 people with clearly specified tasks to achieve.

A simple recipe for organizational success is to have effective leaders occupying these roles and working together in harmony as a team. That is simple enough to say: I am not implying that it is easy either to achieve or to maintain that state of affairs under the pressures of life today. But what is your alternative?

Within each broad level there may be subdivisions. The levels also overlap considerably. But the distinction is still worth making.

Sometimes, however, these three floor levels of the organizational house are disguised by the elaborate façade of hierarchy. A *hierarchy* (from Greek *hierus*, sacred) originally meant a ruling body of priests or clergy organized into orders or ranks each subordinate to the one above. The Greek *archos* was a generic term for a man who was in authority over others, their leader. It comes from a verb which means both to begin and to take the lead. Hence our English word ending *–archy*, which means government or leadership of or by an *arch*. An *archbishop*, for example, is the first or leader among bishops, whereas *monarchy* is rule by one person – a king or emperor.

In Greek phalanxes and Roman formations there were *archoi* of various names among the rank and file. But once battle was joined, formations tended to disintegrate and the natural 'leaders of 10' emerged to rally and lead their comrades forward.

The foundation is the team leader, a truth that continues to evade many large organizations today. 'Ten soldiers wisely led will beat one hundred without a head,' wrote the Greek poet Euripides. A *decanus* in Greek and Latin was the leader of 10 soldiers. From its use in monastic orders for a monk in charge of 10 others, the word comes down to us in the form of dean – the dean of a cathedral or the dean of a university faculty. Our military equivalent is corporal, which derives, like captain, from Latin *caput*, head. *Chief*, coming from *chef*, the French for a head, has the same meaning. Because as humans we stand erect, we tend to assume that a head is a hierarchical model: the head is on top, so it is important. But look at any other animal: the head always goes first – it is the body's leader.

THE FUNCTIONS OF STRATEGIC LEADERSHIP

Although it has been a recent fashion to produce long lists of leadership 'competencies' – some as thick as telephone books – the essential requirements of a leader are simple. The core role at any level refracts into broad functions derived from the three circles model that we saw in Chapter 2. Here, in Figure 3.2, are the three general functions again.

Figure 3.2   *The broad functions of strategic leadership*

This role, of course, has to be fulfilled against a background of a society which has many continuities, but is subject to all manner of changes that constantly impact on each of the three areas and the organization as a whole.

Leadership can be compared to light. Light can be refracted – as Newton demonstrated – into three primary colours: red, green and blue. If you put these three colours into the three circles model (in place of Task, Team and Individual), the intersection triangle in the middle is light.

Using a prism, Newton was then able to refract light into the seven conventional colours of the rainbow: red, orange, yellow, green, blue, indigo and violet. You can think of these colours as representing the seven or eight main functions into which the generic role of leader breaks down.

Working from some first principles of organizations, the generic role of strategic leadership (or *strategia*) refracts into seven colours or functions – in no order of importance:

- Giving direction for the organization as a whole;

- Strategic thinking and strategic planning;

- Making it happen;

- Relating the parts to the whole;

- Building key partnerships and other social relationships;

- Releasing the corporate spirit;

- Choosing and developing leaders for today and tomorrow.

We shall explore in depth these seven key functions together in Part Two. You should then be able to identify some practical ways in which you can improve your effectiveness in each of the seven functions, so that you eventually achieve your personal goal of excellence as a strategic leader.

KEY POINTS

▪ A leader is the sort of person with the appropriate *qualities* and *knowledge* – which is more than technical or professional – who is able to provide the necessary *functions* to enable a team to achieve its task and to hold it together as a working unity. And this is done not by the leader alone but by eliciting the contributions and willing cooperation of all involved.

▪ Organizations need effective leadership at three levels – strategic, operational and team – together with team working between the levels. To achieve this state or condition should be among your top priorities as a strategic leader.

▪ The generic role of leader at the strategic level refracts into seven functions. Most strategic leaders have 'blind spots'. They rate themselves – or are rated highly by others – in some functional areas, but are unaware that they are 'blind' to one or two of the other essential functions.

▪ All leaders need *awareness*, *understanding* and *skill*:

– Awareness. What is going on in the group organization; how the three circles are acting upon each other, for good or ill.

– Understanding. What particular function is required at this particular time.

– Skill. The ability to do what needs to be done both effectively and efficiently.

▪ Nothing can be done without teamwork. One man cannot launch a ship, as the Swahili proverb goes.

If you wish to know a man, give him authority.

Bulgarian proverb

PART TWO

THE SEVEN FUNCTIONS

04

GIVING DIRECTION

Keep the general end in sight while tackling daily tasks.
Chinese proverb

'What is your opinion of Gaius Antonius?' a young Roman of noble family once asked Plutarch.

'He is a man with no aptitude for leadership in any direction, either good or bad,' replied Plutarch. You won't be surprised to learn that Gaius Antonius never made it into Plutarch's *Parallel Lives*, a collection of biographies of prominent Greek and Roman leaders exposing their moral virtues and vices.

Plutarch's reply suggests that there are two simple truths about strategic leadership. First, it is about *the aptitude to lead in a direction* – this way rather than that way. That should come as no surprise to you now, for you will recall that leadership comes from the Anglo-Saxon *laed*, meaning road, path, track or the course of a ship at sea. It is a journey word. In the ancient world the captain of a ship was also the helmsman: his essential function was to steer the ship and its crew safely in a given direction. In order to steer the correct course he needed to have knowledge and experience in the art of navigation.

Secondly, *the direction you lead others can be specified*. You can, for example, lead people forwards or backwards, in the right direction or wrong one, good or bad. Obviously you want to lead your organization forwards, in the right direction, and to good ends.

Here allow me to introduce a distinction between *general* direction and *specific* direction. The latter is – or should be – the result of effective strategic thinking, and it is the subject of the next chapter. General direction, however, is governed by three factors: *purpose, values* and *vision* – in that order of importance.

PURPOSE

Purpose is a very general word, so let me introduce what I mean by it by distinguishing it from its neighbour words: see Table 4.1.

Table 4.1   Purpose, aims and objectives

Purpose	The overarching, general or integrating task of the group or organization.
	Your defined purpose answers the *why* questions – 'Why are we in business?' 'Why are we doing this?' It can signify too the content of value or meaning in what you are doing.
	Human nature craves meaning, and so if your purpose connects with personal and moral values you will not find it difficult to generate a *sense of purpose* in your team – and here *purpose* means *energy*. Your team organization will be under way, like a ship at sea.
	Purpose is not the same as *vision*. A vision is a mental picture of what you want the team or the organization to look like or be in, say, three years' time.

Table 4.1 *Continued*

Aims	You can break purpose down into *aims*, which are open ended but directional. 'To become a better violinist' is an aim. You can have several – 'to improve my skills as a cook', for another example. But you shouldn't have too many, for your time and resources are limited. And that is also true of teams and organizations. So once you have identified purpose, choose aims carefully.
Objectives	*Objectives* are far more tangible, definite, concrete and time bounded. The word comes from a shortening of the military phrase 'objective point'.
	A familiar picture-word or metaphor for objective is *target*, originally the mark at which archers shot their arrows. A target is tangible and visible. You can clearly see the arrows sticking in the outer and inner rings or the bullseye.
	A *goal* is another such picture-word. A football match takes place within clearly defined limits of space and time; players can see instantly if they score a goal. If they are frustrated they can go and kick the goalposts! To score goals in a match or to reach the finishing line in a marathon race calls for prolonged effort and hardship, and those overtones often colour the use of the word 'goal' in ordinary working life.

Moving down the ladder in Figure 4.1, ask: '*How* are we going to achieve the task?' The answer is, by breaking the purpose into the main aims and then the main aims into short- and long-term objectives or goals.

Moving up the ladder, ask: '*Why* are we doing this?' The answer is, to achieve this objective in order to achieve this aim and to satisfy this purpose.

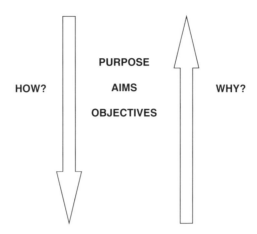

Figure 4.1   *Jacob's ladder model*

Always remember that an objective should be tangible, concrete, limited in time; an aim is less defined but is still fairly substantial rather than abstract; but a purpose may be couched in general or value terms.

THE REASON WHY

The apparently quite simple behaviour of a leader telling a group what to do in fact discloses several distinct levels of mental ability. These cannot be directly associated with the levels of leadership, incidentally, although there ought to be some correlation between them.

Perhaps the key ability for you to focus on first is the ability to break down the general into the particular. Aristotle taught his pupil, the future Alexander the Great, the simple lesson of how to take a general intention and turn it into a specific objective. (That's why Alexander was able to conquer the known world; unfortunately he eventually ran out of both world and time, but that's another story.) All leaders need this skill of quarrying objectives out of aims, and then cutting steps into the objectives so that the objectives can be achieved. Or, as a proverb puts it more colourfully, 'If you're going to eat an elephant you have to do it one mouthful at a time.'

The reverse process – relating the particular to the general – is equally important. Leaders tend naturally to give the reason why something has to be done; bosses just tell you to do it. Answering the question 'why' means connecting it in the group's mind with the larger ongoing aims or purposes.

THE PURPOSE OF BUSINESS

So what does Cadbury think companies are for? 'The fundamental role of a company is to provide the goods and services people want, and to do so efficiently, ethically and profitably,' says Sir Adrian Cadbury, former chairman of Cadbury Schweppes. 'Companies are chartered by society. They have a legal existence; they have benefits; and in return there is an implied contract with society. Companies need to deliver the benefits society expects from them. Why should they have favoured status otherwise?'

On that definition, he says, corporate governance is the job of 'holding the balance between economic and social goals. The aim is to align as neatly as possible the interests of individuals, corporations and society. The incentive for corporations is to achieve their corporate aims and to attract investment. The incentive for states is to strengthen their economies and discourage fraud and mismanagement.'

In the final analysis, he says, 'the character of the company is collectively in our hands. We have inherited its reputation and standing and it is for us to advance them.'

In other words, as one early Cadbury statement of aims so admirably puts it, 'Nothing is too good for the public.'

EXERCISE

Take a few minutes to think about the purpose of your organization, which may or may not be explicitly stated. In either case, write down how *you* understand that purpose. Then take 10–15 minutes to write down your answers to the following questions:

Thinking about your day at work yesterday:

- In what ways did your decisions and actions align with the purpose?
- What stopped you serving this purpose?
- How can you remove these blocks?
- How can you help your team members to reconnect with their sense of purpose?
- What will you do today that is mainstream in respect of the purpose of your organization?

VALUES

'We had our personal differences,' said Winston Churchill, talking about President de Gaulle, 'but we navigated by the same stars.'

Values are the stars you navigate by in life. You will never reach a star – it is not a destination like the port of Rotterdam. But a single star or a constellation can give you direction.

In the plural, values signify the principles or moral standards of a person, group or organization: what is considered to be valuable or important. The assumption is that these are basic beliefs and convictions that govern behaviour.

Values are abstract – you cannot see them and it is sometimes tempting to believe (or act) as if they do not exist until the keel of your ship strikes a submerged iceberg because you have not kept your values in sight.

In other words, there is a moral direction that an organization needs to be moving in. You are accountable for that, too. If you are morally blind it is best to stay away from any role as a strategic leader, because you won't last. As the Latvian proverb says, evil masters do not rule for long.

The reason why that is so is that human nature is fundamentally good. We are born to seek good, to move from fair to good, from good to great. If you cannot lead us in that direction we will look for another leader who can.

VISION

Vision, again, is a general word. It is much bandied about in books and courses on 'transformational' leadership: it has a charismatic, almost mystical, ring to it. As such it has become something of a cliché, a hackneyed or overused word almost drained of meaning. It is, for example, sometimes used merely as a synonym for some aim or goal.

The strong linkage between the concepts of vision and leadership, of course, will always be there. On physical journeys, for example, a leader needs vision in its most basic sense – the ability to see. 'If the blind lead the blind, surely both will fall into a pit,' as the ancient proverb goes.

Vision in non-physical contexts was defined by the Irish satirist and poet Jonathan Swift as 'the art of seeing things invisible'.

Imagination is the name we give to this mental power to call up images, to picture or conceive things that are not actually before the eye or within the experience. And so it may apply to the representation of what is remembered, or of what has never been experienced in its entirety, or indeed of what is actually non-existent. For as humans we have this extra-ordinary and unique faculty to consider actions or events not yet in existence.

In thinking forward into the future we can imagine or picture to ourselves states and conditions that do not exist, that are better than the reality we know now. Vision in this sense may well reflect creative thinking as well as imaginative thinking.

Where an organization or a team, a nation or a community has a common vision of its future being – the desired state or con-dition it holds up before itself even in the dark days – it will also have as a by-product a sense of direction. It will know the difference between moving in one direction rather than another, between progress and regress.

Where there is a vision in this sense you do not have to drive people forwards: the music of the vision *draws* them in a certain direction.

CHECKLIST: GIVING DIRECTION

	Yes	No
1. Are you clear about the purpose of your organization, what it is meant to do and be?		
2. Do all members of your organization understand *why* what they are doing is worthwhile?		
3. Would you say that everyone has a *common* purpose, whatever their roles or responsibilities?		
4. Can you identify and write down the three key values or moral principles that guide your organization?		
5. Do you think that any changes are needed in these values? (If you answer yes, write down the new set of values.)		
6. Have you developed a widely shared vision of what sort of organization you are building for the future?		
7. If so, could you produce for your colleagues a kind of sketch map in words of what it would look like?		

KEY POINTS

▪ Purpose is the *raison d'être*, the reason for being, of an organization. A hospital could be administered much more easily if there were no patients, but would it be a hospital?

▪ Purpose suggests significance. It answers the question *why* – 'Why are we doing this work day in and day out?' – in ways that connect with people's deeper nature.

▪ Values are like stars. They give you direction but you never reach them. But then, as the Spanish writer Cervantes said, 'The road is always better than the inn.'

▪ They include the moral principles, such as truth and integrity, which keep an organization from falling into a pit. 'When the blind lead the way, woe to those who follow' (Honduras).

▪ As a strategic leader you should always keep your eyes on the horizon, for your task is to create tomorrow's organization out of today's – while doing today's work!

▪ Remember that a task without a vision is drudgery; but vision without a task is merely a dream.

Without a vision the people perish.

Book of Proverbs

05

STRATEGIC THINKING AND PLANNING

All men can see the tactics whereby I conquer, but what none can see is the strategy out of which great victory evolved.
Sun Tzu (fourth century BC)

As a strategic leader your prime responsibility is to ensure that your organization is going in the right direction. That sounds simple enough, but it is not always easy to achieve. What *is* the right strategic direction? How or where do you establish it? Why is implementation so difficult?

We can break the problem into two parts: identifying the best strategy and pursuing it to the desired result. Although these two parts in reality are interwoven, it makes sense to separate out the thinking side of it. That is what I call *strategic thinking*.

It is useful, I think, to distinguish between such strategic thinking on the one hand and *strategic planning* on the other. Strategic thinking is thinking about the longer term and the more important ends in any situation, and the pathways that may or may not lead to them.

If and when you can identify such an end or set of ends, and choose among the possible pathways the ones that make most sense, the process of corporate planning can get under way. It doesn't make sense to launch into a strategic planning exercise before your strategic thought has come to some working conclusions, although, believe me, that does happen.

THE MILITARY ANALOGY

Let me remind you that *strategy* in ancient Greek meant the whole art of being an effective commander-in-chief, including leadership, administration and working with allies, as well as knowing how to bring an enemy to battle and what tactics to employ. Strategy, if you like, was the thinking of a *strategos*, a general, and he had a lot to think about apart from the conduct of military operations.

•

As armies have become larger and warfare more complex, strategy is now often contrasted to *tactics* and *logistics*. But strategy is still about what a commander-in-chief, together with his staff and advisers, think is the best way. Strategy usually implies the conceiving and planning of major operations intended to gain the objectives of the war. Tactics are about the handling of forces in the field or in action, under the direction of a commanding officer (operational leader) on the scene.

In the course of time there have been attempts by military thinkers to identify a set of principles for the conduct of a war at the strategic level. In my own view, whatever the merits of studying these principles for aspiring generals they are not readily transferable to fields of human enterprise other than the military. And so I suggest that we have to try to think more generically about strategic thinking. Are there any first principles? Between us we need to discover them, otherwise how shall we be able to teach strategic thinking to ourselves so that we become better at it?

THE NATURE OF STRATEGIC THINKING

In any context – organizational or personal – I suggest that thinking can be described as strategic when it is doing three things: focusing on the important rather than the urgent; the longer term rather than the short term; and all relevant elements or factors in the equation rather than just one. Table 5.1 summarizes these distinctions.

Table 5.1 The nature of strategic thinking

Importance	The starting point is to be able to distinguish between the important, the less important and the unimportant. If it is important it is marked by or possesses weight or consequence. It has evident value, either generally or in particular relation, and often by merely existing.
Longer term	How long is long? That all depends. But *strategic* implies a longer-term perspective rather than the short-term view. Indeed, to think strategically may mean trading short-term gain for long-term advantage.
Multi-factor	Taking all the factors or elements relevant to the overall end into account, not just one – however important that may be.

I see strategic thinking as something that is continuous or recurrent, not something that you sit down, say, once a year and do in a day, giving it no more thought for another year. I am not saying that you should do it all the time – there are, after all, six other leadership functions to bear in mind. But strategy needs to be constantly revisited as change alters your field and affects the positioning of your organization within it.

Frederick R Kappel (1902–94), president and chief executive, and later chairman, of the American Telephone and Telegraph Company, distinguished between *reflective thinking* and *action thinking*:

> I use the term 'reflective' thinking to cover the mental activity required to ask searching (and sometimes embarrassing) questions about the adequacy of the current operation. This kind of thinking can be disturbing to some men at the center of successful action, because they may see it as dealing with remote abstractions, with theories of management that seem impractical, and with visionary speculations about the future. The success of a business today, largely based on action thinking, gives the opportunity to build vitality but it doesn't do the building. For that, reflective thinking is essential.
>
> Looking at the business of the Bell System [*the AT&T monopoly that had provided telephone service in the United States from 1877*], I know we can reach our immediate goals without a great deal of reflective thinking. But doubt that we can build vitality for tomorrow without a lot of it, for this is the way we get deeper understanding of our problems. I make this point because I believe the pressures to meet the problems of the day tend to discourage reflective thinking, and when this happens to a business it will surely lose vitality.

You can see that the enemy of what Kappel calls reflective thinking is that distaste for abstract thinking. Managers see themselves as practical doers, as action oriented, and not as abstract thinkers. As a chief executive, however, you should encourage reflective thinking at all levels of leadership responsibility.

STRATEGIC PLANNING

Strategic thinking has to issue in a strategic *plan* which clears the desk for action; otherwise it degenerates into strategic daydreaming. The process of strategic planning is a two-way and highly interactive one between you as the strategic leader and the operational leaders who head up the 'strategic business units' (as they were first called by General Electric) or their equivalents. What is critically important is the 'one-liners' from the top – simple directives to particular parts of the organization or, in a federal set-up, to organizations within the group – that point the 'part' to an achievable mission which is coherent with, and contributing towards, the overall strategy.

It is not enough to have vision – to see the end or desired result clearly. This must be translated into all the specific statements of long-term goals and medium-term objectives, strategic options, detailed plans, action programmes and budgets that are necessary to make the vision a living reality that is 'owned' at every level of the organization.

MAKING IT HAPPEN

It is essential for the Cabinet to move on, leaving in its wake a trail of clear, crisp, uncompromising decisions. That is what government is about. And the challenge to democracy is to get it done quickly.

Clement Attlee (1883–1967), written when he was Prime Minister of the United Kingdom

This strategic planning process is done differently in every organization and, in large multi-product multinational companies, it still tends to be an immensely complex and time-consuming process involving managers at every level of the organization.

The best course for a strategic leader today is to delegate as much as possible of this process to the operational leaders – the heads of the chief parts that make up the whole. Be an architect rather than a master builder. You should always be able to write your strategic directions in the format of a few broad goals on a piece of paper the size of this page. Encourage others further down the organization to propose other objectives, while creating an expectation that more should be allowed to emerge as things progress.

What your broad goals should do is define the strategic direction of the organization, so that operational leaders work out their own plans and objectives – and propose others – in the light of that flight path. Some 'one-liners', as Sir John Harvey-Jones called them, may provide all the focus that an experienced and professional operational leader who shares the common purpose, values and vision needs. If they just cannot translate the score into great music, they should not be heading up the strings or woodwinds. Look for replacements. It is not your job to lead the violins.

Actually, immensely complex strategic plans are not a good idea, because they offend the principle of flexibility. Here is a parable:

Von Schlieffen was a Prussian Chief of General Staff who died in 1913, but his eponymous plan, revised and updated by his successor, lived on after him. It was an elaborate plan for mobilizing and deploying great armies against France and Russia, using the railway network. France would be knocked out first in a lightning campaign through neutral Belgium to outflank the Maginot Line. Then reinforcements would be sent by train to apply decisive force against Russia. At the eleventh hour in 1914, however, the autocrat of Germany, Kaiser Wilhelm, decided that he only wanted a war against Russia, not France or its ally Britain. His Prussian Chief of Staff, von Moltke, declared that it was quite impossible to change the plan. All the railway timetables were fixed towards either a war against France and Russia or no war at all. The Kaiser eventually gave in. By 1918 over 20 million people had lost their lives as a result.

The trouble with the Schlieffen Plan was that it lacked flexibility. Strategy, as the product of a mind or minds, once incarnated as a plan, is like any other artistic product – a book or poem, a musical composition – in that it can take on a life of its own quite independent of its creator. If the umbilical cord of strategic thinking is cut, the strategic plan may soon become out of date or inappropriate in some form or another.

As a wise general once said, 'A plan is a very good basis for changing your mind.' When it comes to strategic planning, keep the plan as simple as possible, so that it can easily be modified if circumstances demand it. Second, if there are obvious contingencies – something liable to happen as an adjunct to the planned course of action or a possible situation that can be foreseen – build them into the plan.

For unforeseen contingencies make sure that you have something in reserve, just as a wise general always keeps some units out of the first encounter. If the plan itself proves unworkable for really unforeseeable reasons – not the ones you should have foreseen but overlooked or ignored – have a Plan B ready to fall back on.

Flexibility begins in the mind. It should characterize the way you think strategically, not merely the downstream activity of drawing up plans. There is a balance to be struck between flexibility and not abandoning carefully thought-out plans or courses of action lightly. It is a matter of judgement. But it helps to remember that flexibility is essentially about *means* and not about the *end* in view. You should be flexible about means, especially if the differences between them are inconsequential. As the Chinese proverb says, 'It matters not if a cat is black or white as long as it catches mice'.

Some people confuse flexibility with weakness. There is a tradition that emphasizes the strength and indomitable will power of the individual leader. A strong leader who perseveres without a second thought down the path they are committed to after the course has changed is perceived as weak. Even if compelled to change course, a 'strong' leader denies it has happened to avoid the feared accusation of weakness. But such thinking betrays a misconception of strength. It is quite possible to be both flexible and firm.

> You have to hold this balance between flexibility of mind and strength of will, to watch that your strength of will does not become just obstinacy, that your flexibility of mind does not become vacillation. Every man must work this balance out for himself. One word of warning: if you go about reminding yourself that you are a strong man you'd better take a good look at yourself; there's something wrong.
>
> Field Marshal Lord Slim (1891–1970)

Yet it is important that, while being organic, a strategic plan should not be too formless or inchoate. It has to be explicit to be effective and specific enough to require some actions and exclude others.

SOME PRINCIPLES TO BEAR IN MIND

Can strategic thinking be taught? It is certainly an aptitude that can be recognized, and – like all aptitudes – developed by thought, study and practice. Here are some generic principles:

- Selection and maintenance of the aim. This phrase is never far from my mind. It is actually the first or foundation of the Principles of War, but none the worse for that. It is a perennial reminder that you need to be clear about your purpose or end, your aims and objectives. Stay focused; don't get diverted from your carefully chosen course of action without some really compelling reason. It is easy to lose momentum. Be absolutely clear about your aim.

- Strive for simplicity. Complexity, complacency and arrogance are the worst diseases of organizational life. Your task is to understand and grasp the complexity of your situation and then reduce it to the simple.

- Listen for ideas. Listen to the corporate wisdom of the organization if you can find it. Listen especially to those who disagree with you or challenge your views. You need their stimulus to keep thinking clearly.

- All effective strategic thinkers develop their own sets of mental maps. They keep in mind the Big Picture – an overall view of what is going on that is important globally in their field. Make it a priority to keep up to date with what is happening in the world and in your field as well as your organization.

KNOW YOUR FIELD OF ACTIVITY

Another quality common to leaders is their willingness to work hard, to prepare themselves, to know their field of activity thoroughly. I have often heard it said of some individual: 'Oh, he'll get by on his personality.' Well, he may 'get by' for a time but if a charming personality is all he has, the day will come when he will find himself looking for a job.

I never knew President Roosevelt as well as I did some of the other world leaders, but in the few conferences I had with him I was impressed, not only by his inspirational qualities but by his amazing grasp of the whole complex war effort. He could discuss strategy on equal terms with his generals and admirals. His knowledge of the geography of the war theatres was so encyclopaedic that the most obscure places in faraway countries were always accurately sited on his mental map. President Roosevelt possessed personality, but as his nation's leader in a global conflict, he also did his homework – thoroughly.

Dwight D Eisenhower

▩ Do not expect your operational leaders to be fully committed to carrying out the strategic plan unless they have been able to have some input into it.

It is best to think of strategic thinking and strategic planning as an organic function of the organization – or, more accurately, the leadership of the organization. That body of 'thought leadership' is wider than you, wider even than the management hierarchy. Your job is to monitor, guide and direct it, and – at the right time – to put your stamp of authority on it. You and your team will then be free to make it happen.

CHECKLIST: STRATEGIC THINKING AND PLANNING

	Yes	No
1. Does your organization have a strategy that fits its purpose, values and vision?		
2. Do you revise and re-evaluate that strategy in the light of changing circumstances?		
3. Have you developed a strategy that is as simple as possible, rather than complicated?		
4. Is the strategic plan flexible enough for modern conditions?		
5. Have you listened to the strategic ideas, questions and creative thinking from your advisers and senior colleagues?		
6. Are you actively seeking to develop your own knowledge, abilities and range as a strategic thinker?		
7. Could you write down the three chief lessons about strategic thinking and planning you have learnt from others or acquired by experience?		
8. Does your strategic plan include 'success criteria' for measuring its overall results?		

KEY POINTS

▪ As a strategic leader you are the architect of the corporate strategic thinking and planning. That doesn't mean that you have to do all the work yourself.

▪ Wise strategic leaders do not do things if they are not clear about them. Make sure that your strategy is clear. The function of argument with your colleagues is to achieve clarity.

▪ 'Deerhunter, do not waste your arrows on the birds.' This African proverb should serve as a reminder: you should not only select your aim but *maintain* it. Don't dissipate your resources on irrelevant diversions or sideshows.

▪ Leadership is about changing things; creative leadership is about changing them before others do.

▪ 'The more that people share in decisions which affect their working life, the more they tend to be committed and motivated to carry them out.' Never forget that principle when it comes to strategic planning.

▪ Strategic thinking is hard work but it is also fun. It is opening the door to success for all who work with you – your partners – in the organization.

Keep your fears to yourself but share your courage with others.

Robert Louis Stevenson (1850–94)

06

MAKING IT HAPPEN

Between the idea
And the reality
Between the motion
And the act
Falls the Shadow
          T S Eliot (1888–1965), **The Hollow Men (1925)**

These days many strategic leaders, in both private and public sectors of organizational life, are called chief executive – a shortened form of the American title chief executive officer (CEO). To execute means to put into effect, to perform, to carry out what exists in plan or intent – in short, to *make it happen*.

'A log of wood may lie in the river for years but it never becomes a crocodile,' says a trenchant African proverb. Many managers are promoted to the role of strategic leader but lack leadership ability: they are logs, not crocodiles. This functional area of strategic leadership is one of real weakness for them. They can – with help from others – agree purpose, values and vision;

they can even draw up impressive and detailed strategic plans; but *it does not happen*. The vision remains a dream; the strategic plan remains just a piece of paper. Eventually people come to realize that what they hear from their chief executive is the sound of a hollow log, but by then it is too late. Like the dawn, opportunity waits for no organization.

> No one would have doubted his ability to reign, had he never been emperor.
>
> Roman historian Tacitus (AD 56–117), writing about Emperor Galba

Contrast such a useless chief executive with an effective strategic leader. They know that a key part of their role is to oversee the implementation of the strategic plan. It is not their job to conduct the actual business of achieving the common task – that is the responsibility of operational and team leaders. As the Chinese proverb says, 'Behind an able man are always other able men.' But they are in a similar role to an architect, who has an overall responsibility not just for designing and planning a building but also for visiting the site while work is in progress, inspecting it and intervening where necessary.

> My observation on every employment in life is that, wherever and whenever one person is found adequate to the discharge of a duty by close application thereto, it is worse executed by two persons, and scarcely done at all if three or more are employed therein.
>
> George Washington, letter to Henry Knox, 24 September 1792

CONTROLLING

The general name for the leadership function that lies behind the phrase 'making it happen' is *controlling*. Its word origin gives you the best clue as to what it means.

'No one will miss this bag of gold if I slip it under the table. In the account I'll put it down as travel expenses.' In the Middle Ages the royal servants in the various departments of state were not above helping themselves from the till. Hence it was necessary to supervise their accounts of payments and receipts by keeping a duplicate roll. Then you could check or verify payments *contra rotulus*, against that (second) roll.

A contraction of this medieval Latin phrase has given us our modern word *control*. In its wider sense, controlling means checking and directing action once work has started to implement the plan. And in this context the primary function of controlling also includes *coordinating* team efforts and *harmonizing* relations as work proceeds.

Once work has started on a project it is vitally important that you control and coordinate what is being done, so that everyone's energy is turning wheels and making things happen – or most of the organization's energy anyway, for human beings are as inefficient as old steam engines and steam is always escaping one way or another. But most of that synergy or common energy of the group or organization should be fully deployed in implementing the common plan and producing the desired results.

How do you do it? The secret of controlling is to have a clear idea in your mind of what should be happening, when it should occur, who should be doing it and how it should be done. The more effectively you have involved your top team of operational leaders in your planning, the more likely it is that they too will have a similar clear picture of what is required. The ideal is that the team or the individual with whom you are dealing should become *self-directing*, so as to regulate their own performance against standards or the agreed plan. Your aim as a leader is to intervene as little as possible.

> A leader is best
> When people barely know that he exists.
> Not so good when people obey and acclaim him,
> Worst when they despise him.
> Fail to honour people,
> They fail to honour you;
> But of a good leader, who talks little,
> When his work is done, his aim fulfilled,
> They will all say, 'We did this ourselves.'
>
> Lao-Tzu (sixth century BC)

Your object, then, in directing, regulating and restraining is to ensure that the organization's work keeps within bounds or on course. That is the sole criterion of your effectiveness as a controller. You have oversight, which means you should be able to look at the whole picture. If problems crop up, such as obstacles or difficulties in the path of the adopted course, you are then in a good position to help the organization to cope with them.

The stance of a controller at the operational level of leadership is to be where the action is, but observing rather than doing. If you watch a good leader in the execution phase of an exercise or project, their eyes are never still. The pattern of ability here is: *look*, *think* and *intervene* – but only where strictly necessary. Obviously if a safety standard is being ignored and someone is in danger of losing life or limb, your thought processes will be instant. But much of what you see will be below standard or performance (especially if you are inclined to be a perfectionist) and you will have to make a judgement whether or not to intervene.

If you do decide on intervention, the principle to use is the minimum possible exercise of power. If you are at the controls of an ocean-racing yacht, for example, you do not normally have to force the rudder about or attack the crew with a boathook.

In order to get the organization – or a part of it – back on to its agreed course you may only have to touch the controls – a quiet word or even a look can do the trick. As the Arab saying has it, 'Who does not understand a look cannot understand long explanations.' The personal course you have to steer as a leader should take you between the two black rocks of *too much interference* and *lack of direction*. Many a leader is shipwrecked in these foaming straits.

If the plan is going well and the organization is composed of self-direction people, you can sometimes have time to help an individual or a team with their part of the task. Some strategic leaders make the mistake of getting so involved in a piece of work that they forget their responsibility for the whole. You do not see the whole forest if you are busy cutting down a tree – which your woodman could do better than you if only he could get his hands on *his* axe! Setting an example of hard work is always a good idea, as long as it does not detract from your function as director or controller.

CONTROLLING IN ORGANIZATIONS

Controlling implies more than simply being firmly in charge. In organizations it is essential to set up *control systems*, which should be kept as simple as possible. Most organizations that fail exhibit – among other things – poor financial controls. In order to control, a controlling system of checks has to be introduced to give the necessary information.

The function of controlling involves checking against standards and directing the course of work in progress. Coordinating and harmonizing imply that you as leader are watching the team at work, poised to intervene constructively if the need arises, and ensuring that the team is working as a team at its best.

That does not mean you should have no work of your own or never lend a hand. But primarily your responsibility for the whole team effort should come first. If you have performed the foregoing functions well and trained your team, it should become largely *self-controlling*.

Successful organizations are characterized by both delegation of the controlling function right down to the front line, and also by some set of central controlling systems.

DO IT NOW

He slept beneath the moon,
He basked beneath the sun,
He lived a life of going-to-do
And died with nothing done.

Epitaph of James Albery (1838–89)

WHEN THINGS ARE GOING WRONG

'How is it that you spend so much time out of your office?' I once asked the president of Toyota. 'In my home country,' I explained, 'chief executives tend to be more or less invisible like badgers. They inhabit the executive suite of corporate headquarters, sitting behind their desks dealing with paper-work all day or attending meetings. It is as if their business is meetings. They tell me that they haven't got time to get out of head office. Why do you do it so differently?'

'The reason is really very simple,' the president replied with a smile. 'We do not make Toyota cars in my office!'

Apart from being more able to have some two-way communication with those who are doing the actual work, your personal visits can raise morale. The power of your very presence is especially important when things are either going wrong or when there is a danger of that happening and it is all falling apart. At such times what is needed is a positive climate. Your spirit – your calmness – will communicate itself to the group. You can inspire confidence.

If you want your organization to continue working effectively, then fear has to be neutralized, because fear unattended has a paralysing effect – it creates the wrong climate. If you can calm yourself, remaining a still centre in the storm, that calmness will be radiated to others: 'If you can keep your head when all about you are losing theirs and blaming it on you,' as Kipling once wrote. If you can do that, then people will calm down and begin to think and work constructively.

Sometimes a calm leader's appearance on the scene and their very presence can almost magically change the situation. And the opposite is also true, as the Arab proverb reminds us: 'A fearful captain makes a frightened crew.' In his novel *Typhoon* (1902), Joseph Conrad graphically describes the relief of a first mate in a severe gale:

> Jukes was uncritically glad to have his captain at hand. It relieved him as though that man had, by simply coming on deck, taken most of the gale's weight upon his shoulders. Such is the prestige, the privilege, and the burden of command.

In his Cabinet room when he was Prime Minister, Harold Macmillan kept a card in front of him with this sentence in his own handwriting: 'Quiet, calm deliberation disentangles every knot.' That is a good practical saying for any leader to bear in mind.

Military history gives us some vivid examples of what effect a calm, cool and collected strategic leader can have in a real crisis. I think of General Robert E Lee at Gettysburg when he knew the battle was lost. As one officer beside him in that dark hour wrote: 'His face did not show the slightest disappointment, care or annoyance, and he addressed to every soldier he met a few words of encouragement. "All will come right in the end; we'll talk it over afterwards." And to a Brigade Commander speaking angrily of the heavy losses of his men: "Never mind, General, all this has been my fault. It is I who have lost this fight, and you must help me out of it the best way you can."'

THE IMPORTANCE OF TEAMWORK

Remember that organizations are supposed to be human machines for making things happen. If your organization consistently fails to perform – to make things happen – then it is not fit for purpose. You need to go back to the drawing board: re-evaluate its purpose, structure, policies and procedures, personnel, and of course its leadership – beginning with your own leadership. For, as the proverb says, 'There are no bad organizations, only bad strategic leaders.' That is not strictly true, but it at least inoculates you against the common tendency of poor leaders to make excuses, to blame others for their organizational misfortunes.

Once you have connected again with your own essential role as strategic leader and are clear as to why you are being paid such a large salary, you should then – I hope with the help of this book – be ready to make the necessary changes. Don't be afraid of change, for without change there would be no need for strategic leaders. Next, look carefully at your operational leaders. Why are they not performing as the vision and chosen strategy require? Whatever their merits in the past, they may be the wrong people for today and tomorrow. Or they may be the right people. If so, they will respond to some training in the role of being an effective operational leader. Explain what you expect from them, and listen to them when they tell you what they expect from you.

One symptom of a seriously useless operational leader is if they agree to do something, great or small, and *they do not do it*. Not only do they fail to fulfil what was in effect a promise but they neglect to inform you that for one reason or another whatever they said would be done is not going to be done. The chief cause why strategic leaders fail to *make it happen* is that they have tolerated this lack of self-discipline and professionalism among their colleagues and operational leaders.

Remember that your key responsibility is to build a high-performance leadership team – strategic, operational and team leaders – in your organization.

THE EIGHT HALLMARKS OF A HIGH-PERFORMANCE TEAM

Clear, realistic and challenging objectives
The team is focused on what has to be done – broken down into stretching but feasible goals, both team and individual. Everyone knows what is expected of them.

Shared sense of purpose
This doesn't mean that the team can recite the mission statement in unison! Purpose here is energy plus direction – what engineers call a vector. It should animate and invigorate the whole team. All share a sense of ownership and responsibility for team success.

Best use of resources
A high-performance team means that resources are allocated for strategic reasons for the good of the whole. They

are not seen as the private property of any part of the organization. Resources include people and their time, not just money and material.

Progress review
The willingness to monitor their own progress and to generate improvements characterizes excellent teams. These improvements encompass process – *how* we work together – as well as tasks – *what* we do together.

Building on experience
A blame culture mars any team. Errors will be made, but the greatest error of all is to do nothing so as to avoid making any! A wise team learns from failure, realizing that success teaches us nothing and continual success may breed arrogance.

Mutual trust and support
A good team trusts its members to pursue their part in the common task. Appreciation is expressed and recognition given. People play to each other's strengths and cover each other's weaknesses. The level of mutual support is high. The atmosphere is one of openness and trust.

Communication
People listen to one another and build on one another's contributions. They communicate openly, freely and with skill (clear, concise, simple and with tact). Issues, problems and weaknesses are not sidestepped. Differences of opinion are respected. Team members know when to be very supportive and sensitive, and when to challenge and be intellectually tough.

Riding out the storms
In times of turbulent change it is never going to be all plain sailing. When unavoidable storms and crises arise, an excellent team rises to the challenge and demonstrates its sterling worth. It has resilience.

CHECKLIST: MAKING IT HAPPEN

	Yes	No
1. Do you maintain a balance between *controlling* with too tight a rein and giving operational leaders too much freedom to do as they please?		
2. Are you able to coordinate work in progress, bringing all the several parts of the organization into a common, harmonious action in proper relation to each other?		
3. Is your organization noted with customers on account of its control systems in the following areas? – quality of product/service – delivery – keeping costs down – safety		
4. Does your strategic plan have provision for regular progress reviews?		
5. Do you visit all parts of the organization on a regular basis?		
6. Do you always take action if a leader in your organization fails to do what they committed themselves to do?		
7. Do all the individual leaders in the organization work together as a high-performance leadership team?		

KEY POINTS

▪ Making a strategic plan is one thing, making it happen is another. As a strategic leader you are ultimately responsible for *both* these key functions.

▪ You cannot carve rotten wood. Prune out from your organization the dead wood: operational leaders who do not do what they commit themselves to do – and lack the courtesy to inform you why.

▪ A wise general will visit his field commanders, overseeing the implementation of the agreed strategic plan. But you should remember to leave tactics to your operational and team leaders – don't interfere unnecessarily, especially if things are going broadly to plan.

▪ When things are going wrong, your presence should have a calming effect. You may be able to bring more resources to bear in order to solve the problem.

▪ Organizations take their drumbeat from the top. If the executive directors (or their equivalent) work as a team, then you have more than half solved the problem of getting the whole organization to see itself as one great team and to act like one.

▪ One of your major challenges as a strategic leader is to ensure that the calibre and capability of your top executive team match the complexity of its environment, the turbulent seas through which it must navigate the ship.

▪ Whatever its shape or composition, *your* team at the top should have the following hallmarks:

– Clear, realistic and challenging objectives;

– Shared sense of purpose;

– Best use of resources;

– Progress review;

- Building on experience;
- Mutual trust and support;
- Communication;
- Riding out the storms.

Very private advice. Do not send telegrams about your doings. Ask to be left alone. Results speak louder than words.

Lord Wolseley advises General Gordon upon his arrival in Khartoum, 1884

07

RELATING THE PARTS TO THE WHOLE

Dust as we are, the immortal spirit grows
Like harmony in music; there is a dark
Inscrutable workmanship that reconciles
Discordant elements, makes them cling together
In one society.

William Wordsworth (1770–1850),
The Prelude, *Book 1*

One major issue in all organizations is *getting the right balance between the whole and the parts*. Therefore the fourth generic function of a strategic leader is to create harmony: to bring together the 'discordant elements' into 'one society'.

Alfred P Sloan who, along with Pierre Du Pont, had an immense influence on corporate organization in the United States, saw that as the key issue for working out his relations with the management team. Writing in *My Years with General Motors* (1964), he expressed it thus: 'Good management rests on a reconciliation of centralization and decentralization, or "decentralization with coordinated control".' For 'centralization' here read *whole*, and for 'decentralization' read *part*. Sloan's solution, as he hinted in his last phrase, is *both–and*: decentralize as much as you can but maintain some essential control from the centre.

That sounds simple but in practice it is not easy to achieve. No formula exists, whatever the popular pundits or gurus on 'organizational behaviour' may say. As a strategic leader you may have to be able to think it out for yourself and make some flexible adjustments as life changes. As Sloan continued:

> There is no hard and fast rule for sorting out the various responsibilities and the best way to assign them. The balance which is struck ... varies according to what is being decided, the circumstances of the time, past experience, and the temperaments and skills of the executive involved.

UNITARY AND FEDERAL ORGANIZATIONS

The relation of the whole to the parts as a perennial issue applies in both *unitary* and *federal* organizations. For there are unitary organizations, the ones that resemble your body and there are federal ones, which are more like your family.

In the political field, federal (from the Latin *foedus*, compact or league) set-ups are composed of political units that surrender their individual sovereignty to a central authority but retain limited residuary powers of self-government. Power is distributed between that central authority and its constituent territorial units. The degree to which they are integrated varies from a *union*, where there is virtually one political identity, to a loose *federation* that functions more like an alliance whose members can choose to leave if they wish. You may be familiar with the debates that have taken place in Europe about the nature of the European Union. Does having a single currency and a single military force constitute steps towards a strong federalist super state on the model of the United States?

Unitary organizations tend to resemble armies in that you can theoretically tell people what to do and they will do it. In modern jargon they are 'command and control organizations', although these days for reasons of political correctness they may pretend to be otherwise.

In federal organizations it is all very different. As the federal leader you can lead but you cannot command. When he was Secretary-General of the United Nations – an archetypal federal organization – Dag Hammarskjöld both reminded himself in his private notebook of this fact and also set before himself the highest ideal of leadership:

> Remember that your position does not give you the right to command. It only lays upon you the duty of so living your life that others may receive your orders without being humiliated.

Beneath the surface in both unitary and federal organizations you can identify the perennial and ever-present issue of the relation of the whole to the parts. That in turn is a reflection of the still deeper relation between the values of *order* and *freedom*. They appear to be opposites and there can certainly be tensions between them. But ultimately they belong together as two eyes are joined in sight. For the true function of order is to create freedom.

HARMONY AT WORK

Where all leaders – not just those at strategic levels – are committed to the whole as well as to their particular part, and where each fulfils their role with all the qualities of a good leader, the organization is dancing. The teamwork of the leaders produces an effect that is best described as *harmony* – the Greek word *harmos*, joint, also gives us words like *arm*. All the arms or parts move and work together in a pleasing and even graceful cooperation like the chords of a musical composition or dancers in a chorus line.

In this respect a great orchestra is a strong metaphor illuminating that underlying concept of organization that all organizations must express. The parts are the individual players, grouped together in teams – strings, woodwind, brass and percussion, each with its own 'first' player or leader. In rehearsal and performance a conductor is the operational leader, whose conducting holds the teams together in an artistically expressive interpretation of the composer's score. The conductor – from the Latin word for one who leads people together or jointly – provides both direction in the performance and cohesion in the orchestra.

This key function of relating the parts to the whole can be also expressed as *organizing* – not as a 'one-off' action but as a continuous activity: something that you are doing all the time in one form or another.

Organizing is the function of arranging or forming into a coherent unity or functional whole. It can suggest systematic planning as well, but that is a function we have already discussed in Chapter 5.

But more importantly, organizing means the structuring that has to be done if people are to work in unity, with each element making its proper contribution. It is essentially concerned with getting right the relation of the whole to the parts. It is a manifestation of perhaps a deep human impulse to impose or bring order in place of chaos. Order is the value that lies behind society, just as freedom is the value that lies behind the individual. To repeat the point, a balance needs to be struck in any group or organization between order and freedom.

REVIEWING YOUR ORGANIZATIONAL STRUCTURE

An organization is by definition the end result of the function of organizing. It is finished, complete and unalterable. Well, is it? Of course it is none of those things in reality, but we tend to make assumptions that this is the case.

An organization is indeed sometimes the product of another person's organizing activity. These days it is more likely to be a committee that does the organizing. Some old and venerable kinds of organization, such as churches and armies, have structures that have lasted centuries, modified but essentially unchanged. The fact that they have withstood the test of time may well be evidence that they are sound, but you cannot take that for granted. Whether the structure you are working in is the product of a single leader, a committee or a tradition, you should not assume that it is perfect either in the sense of being completely finished or in the sense of being without serious fault or blemish.

For it is *people* who did the organizing, and they are always fallible. They may have organized, for instance, with a particular interpretation of the enduring purpose in mind, or in light of a given technology, or assuming a certain level of education or training among members of the organization. The *situational* factors are changing and therefore as a leader in an organization you will need to examine the function of organizing in one way or another.

Assuming that the organization is not as hard as concrete but is organic – growing and developing or contracting according to the situation – your organizing ability will be constantly in play, introducing changes or modifications to the system of ways of doing things. From time to time it is advisable to carry out a survey of the structure of the organization.

You do not want to make changes in this basic structure too often, for no organization (like the individual person) can stand too much change all at once. If you make a major organizational change and get it wrong, you are stuck with the consequences for the next five years – longer, maybe, if it is a very big organization. So it is important to get it right.

Providing you take the three circles model as your guide, you can undertake this structural survey without too much difficulty, especially if you set up a small but representative steering group to work with you. The key is to ask yourself the right questions. Some suggestions are outlined in Figure 7.1 and Table 7.1.

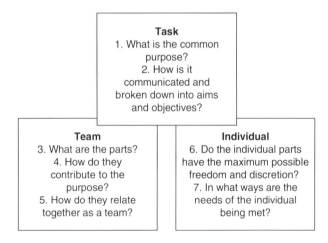

Task
1. What is the common purpose?
2. How is it communicated and broken down into aims and objectives?

Team
3. What are the parts?
4. How do they contribute to the purpose?
5. How do they relate together as a team?

Individual
6. Do the individual parts have the maximum possible freedom and discretion?
7. In what ways are the needs of the individual being met?

Figure 7.1   *Three circles diagram, substituting squares for circles*

Whether you start at the top and work downwards, or vice versa, it is important to be systematic about it. You are trying to see how the pieces of the jigsaw fit together at present, and to collect and collate ideas on how a better structure and method of working together might look.

Table 7.1   Surveying your organization

Question	Notes
1. What is the common purpose?	Besides studying statements of purpose, look at what the organization is actually doing. How does it spend its time and money?
2. How is it communicated and broken down into aims and objectives?	This should lead you into the communication and decision-making processes, vital areas in any organization.
3. What are the parts?	Identify the main groups and subgroups. These are often divided between line (or operations) and staff (or functions), eg finance, sales. How many levels of leader are there?
4. How do they contribute to the purpose?	If they do not make a significant contribution they should not be there.
5. How do they relate together as a team?	Does tribal war exist between the different divisions, or do they cooperate harmoniously together? How well do they communicate with each other on a lateral basis?
6. Do the individual parts have the maximum possible freedom and discretion?	Is decision making pushed down as far as it will go, or is it heavily centralized? Do the main parts or units have sufficient freedom to use their initiative and creativity?
7. In what ways are the needs of the individual being met?	This will take you into systems of remuneration, personnel policy and maybe relations with trade unions.
8. Do the circles overlap sufficiently?	You will soon find out how far the circles overlap in the minds of employees. Is the overlap sufficient to provide and maintain high morale in spite of difficulties?
9. How are tensions between the three circles resolved?	This will take you into the consultative system, disciplinary procedures and the methods for dealing with disputes.

At the lowest level you should search out the answers to the question 'How large or small should the primary group or groups be in this industry?' A good guideline is to establish how many people one person can supervise in light of the factors shown in Table 7.1.

The Roman army, like the Israelites, operated with a primary group of 10 soldiers led by a *decanus* (as I mentioned in Chapter 3, hence our word 'dean'). Football and cricket teams consist of eleven players. However simple the task in technological terms, the span of control of a team leader should probably not exceed 10 or 12 people. This refers to the number who are directly responsible to any given leader, and who therefore constitute their team.

STARTING AT THE TOP

In the Bible, Jethro was the father-in-law of Moses. He should be regarded as the patron saint of all management consultants! He certainly gave Moses some good advice, after the exodus of the 12 tribes of Israel from Egypt, on the need for an accountable structure. One day, while the tribes of Israel were in the desert, he saw Moses sitting with people crowding around him from morning till evening, counselling them and solving disputes.

'This is not the best way to do it,' said Jethro. 'You will only wear yourself out and wear out all the people who are here. The task is too heavy for you; you cannot do it by yourself. Now listen to me...'

Jethro told Moses that he must get his priorities right and put the work that only he could do – his role as a prophet – first. How could he make time to do that?

'You must yourself search for capable, God-fearing men among all the people; honest and incorruptible men,' Jethro told him. 'Then appoint them as leaders of the people – over units of 1,000, of 100, of 50 and 10. They shall sit as a permanent court for the people; they must refer difficult cases to you but decide simple cases themselves. In this way your burden will be lightened, and they will share it with you. If you do this, God will give you strength, and you will be able to go on. And, moreover, this whole people will here and now regain peace and harmony.'

Moses was a leader with humility, which always includes being open to criticism and constructive suggestions. We are told that he did all that Jethro asked of him.

You may have noticed in the passage above that Jethro divided each group of 100 into two groups of 50, so that the leader in charge of each 100 had only two leaders reporting to him. In my opinion that is too few. I like to think that this is why, eventually, 'Moses sent his father-in-law on his way, and he went back to his own country.'

For if you have only two people reporting to you, it is perfectly possible, if you work hard, to do their jobs for them. But if you have seven or eight people reporting to you, the structure is encouraging you to delegate. As a rule of thumb, aim to build a structure of working groups composed of between five and 10 people. Such a policy will insure you against the common mistake of building into the structure too many levels of leadership or management. Albert Einstein's wise words certainly apply to organization: 'Everything should be made as simple as possible but not simpler.'

The organizational structure is the bony skeleton of the organization. It should be functional in terms of the purpose, so that it adequately supports the muscle power and a robust communication system. Simplicity must be a hallmark at every level. Finally, it will work only if its cells and organs are free and flexible enough to be realigned at short notice to meet the challenges of a rapidly changing environment.

It is important always for you as a strategic leader to keep coming back to *purpose* (see Chapter 4). A hospital exists to make sick people better, whatever ends are pursued by some of the staff working there. There is always a truth about why organizations are there – or what they should be doing – but it is often a great intellectual struggle to achieve and maintain clarity on the matter. This is especially true in a rapidly changing social, technological and economic situation. Changes in the methods or means by which the purposes are achieved are then demanded. Sometimes they call into question the fundamental purpose of the organization.

It follows that if you are unable to define the purpose or to formulate any vision for the organization – what it should look like in three years' time – you will not be able to appraise its present structure or embark upon any meaningful organizational development.

It often requires considerable courage, decisiveness and determination to set about reorganizing to achieve the purpose more effectively in the present and in the future. For organizations tend to resist change. They like to live in the past, usually the recent past. The need for group cohesiveness – to remain together just as we are – is a powerful one. It can work against the leader as well as for them. Moreover, no organization can handle too much change all at once. As persons we have a very basic human need for a balance of continuity and change in our lives. And as we grow older – individuals or organizations – continuity tends to win out over change. As a strategic leader you need political acumen to bring about the necessary changes with the minimum disruption, and with a proper respect for valued continuities with the past. But if you do not tackle the agenda of change you are no leader.

A GOOD STRATEGIC LEADER ALWAYS DELEGATES

From the story of Moses above, it is clear that delegating and organizing are closely related. Jethro advised Moses to delegate and that meant setting up an organization. To delegate means to give a colleague the authority and freedom to handle certain matters on their own initiative, with the confidence that they can do the job successfully. It is not to be confused with abdication:

> Delegation. Telling a subordinate the results required and giving them the authority – 'Do it your way and ask for help if required.'

> Abdication. Relinquishing responsibility for the job – 'Do it any way you like but don't ask for help if it goes wrong.'

Sometimes people assume that an individual (or an organization) can delegate more at will. But delegation can only happen effectively if, for example, the right staff have been selected and trained for the job. For delegation to happen, an organization needs to pursue definite policies over selection, training, appraising performance and career planning.

Remember that you should not delegate unless you are willing to give the person concerned the necessary authority to do the job, matched with your supportive trust in them. Be available to discuss progress or to help with any problems they cannot deal with themselves. Grip your desk hard and do not interfere! Accept the fact that the job will be done differently from the way that you would have done it, but will still fall within the bounds of success. Such effective delegation serves a twofold purpose: it frees you for constructive work on larger projects, and it is a necessary technique for furthering the growth and development of subordinates. Make sure that the person knows what results are expected of them and make them accountable for their performance.

ORGANIZING YOURSELF

Sure signs of whether or not you are capable of executing the function of organizing lie in your own life. Have you got the balance right between the whole and the parts in your own life? A good indicator is whether or not you are good at organizing your own time.

It is essential for you as a strategic leader to make time to think, both about the present and the future. That means in the first place an awareness of the value of time and the economical use of it. 'Ask me for anything,' Napoleon used to say, 'except for time.' He knew that he had only 24 hours a day like anyone else, but he used his time most effectively. Do you?

MAKING TIME TO THINK

What advice can be offered to a leader? He must discipline himself and lead a carefully regulated and ordered life. He must allow a certain amount of time for quiet thought and reflection; the best times are in the early morning, and in the evening. The quality, good or bad, of any action which is to be taken will vary directly with the time spent in thinking; against this, he must not be rigid; his decisions and plans must be adaptable to changing situations. A certain ruthlessness is essential, particularly with inefficiency and also with those who would waste his time. People will accept this, provided the leader is ruthless with himself...

Most leaders will find there is so much to do and so little time to do it; that was my experience in the military sphere. My answer to that is not to worry; what is needed is a quiet contemplation of all aspects of the problem, followed by a decision – and it is fatal to worry afterwards.

Field Marshal Viscount Montgomery (1887–1976)

Here are some practical suggestions to help you to make the best use of your time at work. Health check yourself against this 10-point programme once a month for the next six months.

1. **Develop a personal sense of time**
   Do not rely on memory or assume that you know where your time goes. For one or two weeks keep a record. Become more aware of the value of your time and resolve to use it well.

2. **Identify your longer-term goals and policies**
   The clearer you are about your longer-term ends the easier you will find it to identify your priorities. Policies are decisions about principles: they help you to make many daily decisions without having to waste too much time on them.

3. **Make middle-term plans**
   You should be able to translate fluently *purpose* into *aims*, and *aims* into *objectives* (see Chapter 4). Plan your work on aims and objectives in terms of opportunities and desired results, priorities and deadlines.

4. **Plan the day**
   Make a list of what you want to do each day. Arrange it or mark it in some order of priority. Learn to say no, otherwise you will become merely a slave to the priorities of others.

5. **Make best use of your best time**
   Your best time is when you do your best work. Where possible, always use it for important tasks. Have some planned quiet periods for creative thinking.

6. **Organize your administrative work**
   Work out systems for handling paperwork, dealing with e-mails and making telephone calls, so that you do not fragment your day. Make administration your servant and not your master.

7. **Manage meetings**
   Work out the agenda carefully, allotting time for each item. Start on time and end on time. Use your skills as a leader to make meetings both businesslike and enjoyable.

8. **Delegate effectively**
   Where possible, delegate as much administrative responsibility as you can. The reason for doing so is to free yourself for exercising the kind of leadership that your position requires.

9. **Make use of committed time**
   Committed time is time given over to specific purposes, such as travel. Use waiting time or travelling time to think, plan, read or make calls.

10. **Manage your health**
    Time management is primarily about the *quality* of your time, not about its *quantity*. Follow common-sense guidelines over sleep, diet, exercise and holidays. Achieve a balance between work and private life that works for you and keeps you free from the toxic kinds of stress.

To summarize, organizing is the function of arranging parts into a working order. 'Structure is a means for attaining the objectives and goals of an institution,' writes Peter Drucker. This is no more than another application of the three circles model. The end result is that you should be able to find and maintain – doubtless with some juggling – the optimum balance between the parts and the whole.

At *group level* you may have to organize for results by setting up *subgroups*. At *organization level*, however, exercising this leadership function may mean introducing *structural changes* to respond to changes in the task, technology or the environment. This chapter contains a guide for carrying out a survey of your own organization, based upon common-sense principles.

Bringing about the changes will, of course, require considerable powers of leadership.

To be effective as a leader you should be able to organize your own work. You should become especially good at managing your time, for it is your most precious resource. You need *time to think* and *time for people*.

It is not enough to be busy. The question is: What are you busy about?

Henry Thoreau, American author and poet (1817–62)

CHECKLIST: RELATING THE PARTS
TO THE WHOLE

	Yes	No
1. Are you clear on the purpose of the organization and how the various parts of it work together to achieve that end?		
2. Is there an effective system for staffing the organization?		
3. Do you carry out regular surveys of the organization to check:		
– the size of all working groups?		
– the number of management levels?		
– the growth of unnecessary complexity?		
– line and staff cooperation?		
– that the communication systems are working properly?		
4. Do you have solid grounds for believing that the balance between centralization and decentralization is about right?		
5. Do you agree that reorganizing the organization too often will only breed disorder and confusion?		
6. Have you got the right balance between the various parts of your life and the whole?		
7. Are there ways in which you could organize your personal and working life, eg how you deal with your personal administration, in order to be a more effective leader?		
8. Do you delegate sufficiently?		
9. Can you identify at least three steps you can take in order to become a better organizer of your time?		

KEY POINTS

▨ As a strategic leader one of your key functions is to create and maintain the right organization for your particular kind of business. The essential principle is to strike the optimum balance between the parts and the whole, between decentralization and centralization.

▨ Bear in mind the concept in political theory of *subsidiarity*: the principle that a central authority (the whole) should have only a subsidiary function and perform only tasks or make decisions which cannot be performed or made at local level (the parts). In other words, the centre is there to serve the parts – not the other way about.

▨ Whenever you get lost as a leader always go back to the three circles model, for it will never fail you. Here it reminds you that it is the nature of the common *task* that should determine the structure of the *team* – in this case, *organization*. If elements of the *task* change, then the model tells you to look at the effects of that change on the other two circles. You will, for example, need to re-evaluate your organizational structure. Don't neglect the effects on individuals either.

▨ If there is a dynamic harmony between parts and whole, more will be achieved in the area of the common *task*.

▨ In order to organize others you need to be well organized yourself. Good administration is the servant of good leadership.

▨ If you cannot master time you will not have time to think or time for people – time, in fact, to lead.

Even a goat and ox must keep in step if they are to plough together.

African proverb

08

BUILDING PARTNERSHIPS

When spiders' webs unite, they can tie up a lion.

Ethiopian proverb

Among the transferable skills of a strategic leader that Socrates identified is attracting allies and helpers. Here I shall call it *building partnerships* – the fifth generic function of strategic leadership.

In 1940 Britain stood alone in the Second World War against the might of Nazi Germany under Hitler. Without major allies it was a war that Britain could never win, nor even perhaps survive. A key aim for Britain's national leader and in effect commander-in-chief of its forces, Winston Churchill, was to bring its natural ally, the United States, into the war on Britain's side. The Japanese attack on Pearl Harbor in December 1941 finally brought that about. Russia also had no option but to join the Allies after being attacked by Hitler in 1941, and together the Allied forces eventually overcame the Axis powers – Germany, Italy and Japan.

As this story illustrates, alliances of nations and their armed forces have been a fact of history. But history also shows that alliances are notoriously difficult to manage. The leadership challenge for Churchill – the fifth strategic leadership function – was to establish harmonious relations with his opposite numbers in America and Russia – President Roosevelt and the redoubtable Stalin. The latter's name in Russian means 'man of steel', which suggested that he would not be the easiest man to do business with. British and American generals, such as Montgomery and Eisenhower, who commanded the military operations in the field, also at their level had to learn to work together in harness.

An *ally* is simply a person, group or organization who helps and supports another. We all have allies or friends in this wide sense, but sometimes we think it wise or politic to formalize such a relation. In personal life marriage is an example. Nations enter into treaties – agreements formally concluded and ratified between different states. So do organizations. The Channel Tunnel, for example, was constructed by a consortium of British and French business companies.

It requires good judgement on your part as a strategic leader as to when and where to enter into such associations or consortiums. But there are some principles to bear in mind.

THE THREE CIRCLES MODEL

So far we have applied the three circles model mainly to what could be called 'inside the egg' issues – to teams working within a given organization, or to the organization itself. But it also applies to alliances 'outside the egg' as well. It tells us, for example, how important it is to *define the task*.

THE FIRST GULF WAR

When Saddam Hussein's Iraqi army invaded Kuwait in 1990 a military alliance was formed to evict the Iraqis from the country under the auspices of the United Nations.

In the event, that objective was easily and swiftly achieved. It then became feasible for the allied army – if it wanted to do so – to complete the job by marching up the road to Baghdad and overthrowing Saddam Hussein. Why did it not happen?

In the three circles model, Task and Team circles overlap. Given the task of evicting the Iraqis from Kuwait, a team of 19 nations came together in order to achieve that specific and limited task. Had the task been changed – for opportunistic reasons – to march on Baghdad and bring about a regime change, the existing team would simply have disintegrated.

You can see that a precision on clarity in *defining the common task* is necessary if you want to enjoy successful alliances or partnerships. You must know what the task entails and what it doesn't entail. Britain's alliance with Russia in the Second World War, for example, was certainly in the self-interest of both in the sense that both were absolutely agreed on the necessity of victory in Europe. Beyond that point – when it came to rebuilding Europe – there was no agreement and the Allies fell apart.

The principal necessary conditions for a successful alliance or partnership, then, is a shared common aim. The attainment of the end in view, of course, needs to be strongly in the interests of both parties, however they define their interests. If the potential contributions of the partners to the common end are complementary, like those of team members in a real team, so much the better. For example, the Romans had an army that was strong in infantry but weak in cavalry. Therefore the republic formed a series of alliances – informal and formal

– with nations who could supply Roman armies with units of mounted troops and archers.

SOCIAL RELATIONS IN GENERAL

As the strategic leader you need to build – or maintain – not only good relations with partners and allies in your field of business but also with society as a whole. Organizations of all sizes are like fish that swim in a great sea. Some of the more managerial chief executives are content if their organizations comply with the law and no more. As a strategic leader, however, you should aspire to a more positive relation with the social environment.

The function of building partnerships, then, is rather like ripples produced when you throw a stone in a pond: it moves out in ever-widening circles: local neighbourhood, region, nation, world, the natural environment of the earth. In all these 'circles' your organization should be on the positive rather than the negative side of the balance sheet.

CHECKLIST: BUILDING PARTNERSHIPS

	Yes	No
1. Do you now see building partnerships as one of the key functions in your role as strategic leader?		
2. Do you balance the time you spend in the organization and the time you spend outside the organization building strategic relations with key players – such as allies, customers, suppliers?		
3. Could your organization achieve more if you joined forces with other partners?		
4. If you consider your products and services, your employment policies and effects on the environment, is your organization socially responsible?		
5. Does your organization confer benefits other than employment upon its local communities?		
6. Does your organization work well with colleagues from other organizations, nations or cultures?		

KEY POINTS

▓ The African concept of *ubuntu* means 'A person is a person because of other persons.' Your organization is a corporate person, and it, too, only exists and grows in relation to others.

▓ The relations of your organization with others – often in time-limited consortiums – may be vitally important. They matter as necessary conditions for business success.

▓ The professional reputation of your organization among its peers and the estimation in which it is generally held in society are assets of strategic importance. They also are a source of considerable pride to the people that work in the organization.

▓ Whenever you enter into partnerships, or work in mixed teams of 'insiders' and 'outsiders', use the three circles model to clarify:

– What is our common *task*?

– How can we best work together as a *team*?

– How can each *individual* (part or organization) give of their best?

▓ Always take seriously the interests of your partner or ally. Make sure that they are getting their share of benefit from the mutual enterprise. Make it a win–win story.

We cannot live only for ourselves. A thousand fibers connect us with our fellow men; and among those fibers, as sympathetic threads, our actions run as causes, and they come back to us as effects.

Herman Melville, American novelist (1819–91)

09

RELEASING THE CORPORATE SPIRIT

*The task of leadership is not to put greatness into humanity,
but to elicit it, for the greatness is there already.*
**John Buchan (1875–1940),
British novelist and politician**

Ibn Khaldun was a famous Islamic scholar in the late Middle
Ages – he died in 1406. A philosopher and historian, he once
spent six weeks in the tents of the Mongol ruler, Tamerlane,
who conquered Persia, northern India and Syria. Ibn Khaldun
talked daily with him. 'One of the greatest and mightiest of
kings,' he said of his host. As to Tamerlane's legendary knowledge, charisma and powers of magic and sorcery: 'In all this
there is nothing; it is simply that he is highly intelligent and
discerning, addicted to debate about what he knows and also
about what he does not know.'

Ibn Khaldun wrote a monumental seven-volume history of the world. In the first volume he came up with a new idea to explain the emergence and decline of tribes or nations. It was nothing to do with the effect on history of great leaders such as Tamerlane. Ibn Khaldun's big new idea was that human beings are made to cooperate. Central to success in cooperation is *asabiyah* or 'group feeling'. Having more *asabiyah* makes one group superior to another. The leader who can then command *asabiyah* to best effect will be stronger than his rivals, and will even be able to form new dynasties, new states.

But, as Ibn Khaldun's history shows, success ultimately breeds luxury and degeneration in the sedentary existence, *asabiyah* weakens, and the urban world becomes exposed to those peoples, usually in the nomadic world, who can command greater *asabiyah*.

ASABIYAH

There is no real equivalent that I can find in English to the Arabic word *asabiyah*. It probably encompasses what we would call group cohesiveness, *esprit de corps* (French for 'spirit of the body'), ethos, morale, confidence, discipline – everything that makes a group a whole that is more than the sum of its parts with an identity of its own. Everything that gives it power and direction – what the French call *élan*, energy and confidence.

Ibn Khaldun does make a connection with the leader's role, but his main emphasis is upon the *group* and its decisive property of group feeling. You can understand why some Western writers have hailed him as the father of social psychology.

Ten soldiers wisely led,
Will beat a hundred without a head

Euripides (fifth century BC)

That is true enough, but the *asabiyah* of the 10 soldiers, not to mention their training and skill, is a factor that is often overlooked.

Personally, on reflection I find that I agree more and more with Ibn Khaldun's message. Leaders depend far more than we tend to think these days on the *asabiyah* of their team. Consider this remarkable observation by the famous author of the first English Dictionary, Dr Samuel Johnson:

THE BRITISH SOLDIER

Doctor Samuel Johnson considered that the special characteristic of the British soldier is a species of 'plebeian magnanimity'. His greatness of heart is exhibited not only in his bravery, but in the qualities he expects in his officers. He relies on them to lead [him], and they on their part are quite satisfied that [he] will follow [them]. It is not that the British soldier lacks initiative, but he considers his [officers'] leadership a tribute to his own loyalty and *esprit de corps*. 'In the case of other nations,' said Doctor Johnson, 'the officers do not lead their men but follow behind to ensure that there is no skulking to the rear.'

Cyril Field, *Old Times Under Arms* (1939)

Johnson is in effect saying that the British regiments in the mid-18th century had a very strong and distinctive *asabiyah*. It was demonstrated by their fighting spirit but also by their attitude to leaders. They expected their officers to lead them from the front; providing they did so they would always follow them. Johnson makes it sound like an arrangement.

If you have the right attitude to leadership you should see it as one job among many other important ones, and yourself as the 'first companion'.

A SENSE OF PARTNERSHIP

I made the soldiers partners with me in the battle. I always told them what I was going to do, and what I wanted them to do. I think the soldiers felt that they mattered, that they belonged.

Field Marshal Montgomery (1887–1976)

As a strategic leader your task – as John Buchan says at the head of this chapter – is not to put greatness into people, as if you were filling up a car with petrol. See it differently: the greatness is there already. You are there to elicit it. Not for your own ends or interests, but in pursuit of a common purpose that has real value. That should be your vision of people as a leader; that is how you should see your organization.

The world's problems are great, and maybe the problems in your organization are formidable too. But the reservoir of human spirit is infinitely larger. Unlock the greatness of the human spirit by leading from the front.

RELEASING CORPORATE ENERGY

I lead by example and persuasion and a hell of a lot of hard work. Not on the basis of power or authority. My skills are to help a large number of people to release their energies and focus themselves. It is switching on a lot of people and helping them achieve a common aim. People only do things they are convinced about. One has to create conditions in which people want to give of their best.

The board of directors should be, in Nelson's phrase, a 'band of brothers'. We should be so aware of one another's views that any one of us could act for the lot of us.

Sir John Harvey-Jones (1924–2008), writing as chairman and chief executive of Imperial Chemical Industries

---

THE FORCE OF PURPOSE

Remember that purpose can also be regarded as a form of energy, somewhat like gravity, as well as being another word for your long-term or ultimate aim. Aims arise, we could say, when purpose is directed and harnessed. Purpose here is energy plus direction – engineers call it a vector. It is comparable to being under way.

You will be familiar now with the idea that leadership is about showing the way – the path or road ahead. In the nautical context, *way* also implies the power that is moving a ship forward. So we talk about a ship as being 'under way'. To lose way, on the other hand, is to lose momentum when sailing; to 'gather way' is to pick up speed again. We talk of a project as being 'now well under way'.

ENCOURAGING TWO-WAY COMMUNICATION

At times I received advice from friends, urging me to give up or curtail visits to troops. They correctly stated that, so far as the mass of men was concerned, I could never speak, personally, to more than a tiny percentage. They argued, therefore, that I was merely wearing myself out, without accomplishing anything significant, so far as the whole army was concerned. With this I did not agree. In the first place I felt that through constant talking to enlisted men I gained accurate impressions of their state of mind. I talked to them about anything and everything: a favourite question of mine was to inquire whether the particular squad or platoon had figured out any new trick or gadget for use in infantry fighting. I would talk about anything so long as I could get the soldiers to talk to me in return.

I knew, of course, that news of a visit with even a few men in a division would soon spread throughout the unit. This, I felt, would encourage men to talk to their superiors, and this habit, I believe, promotes efficiency. There is, among the mass of individuals who carry the rifles in war, a great amount of ingenuity and initiative. If men can naturally and without restraint talk to their officers, the product of their resourcefulness becomes available to all. Moreover, out of the habit grows mutual confidence, a feeling of partnership that is the essence of *esprit de corps*. An army fearful of its officers is never as good as one that trusts and confides in its leaders.

General Dwight D Eisenhower (1890–1969)

Purpose has the overtone of *significance*. Whether you use it for the desired end of your endeavours or for the *esprit de corps* which animates a team or organization, it has the connotation of importance or meaning. That is why it is the golden key that unlocks the human spirit – the greatness within.

CHECKLIST: RELEASING THE CORPORATE SPIRIT

	Yes	No
1. Have you had experience of work groups or organizations with different levels of *asabiyah*, group feeling?		
2. Do you agree that human nature is fundamentally good?		
3. 'The human spirit has a greatness in it that enables people on occasion to do extraordinary things.' Would you agree with this statement?		
4. Have you ever known a leader who seemed to be able to release the greatness in people?		
5. Which of these statements applies more to you: – I do not trust people until they have proved themselves to be trustworthy. – I trust people until such a time as they show themselves to be untrustworthy.		
6. Have you now a clear idea of what your organization expects of its strategic, operational and team leaders?		

KEY POINTS

- As the Scottish proverb says, 'The clan is greater than the chief.' A critical factor about teams or organizations is their *asabiyah*, group feeling or power. The leader who can command it to best effect will be the stronger.

- A driving force of purpose is another word for *asabiyah*. It links the ultimate *end* of our activities with the energy or power it releases in a group. Without significance – some moral value, importance or meaning – a purpose is not a *real* power.

- It is that element of significance in purpose – a sense of the importance of what we are doing – that releases the human spirit. That is why Shakespeare called it 'the very life-blood of our enterprise' (*Henry IV, Part 1*).

- 'As you are, so will your rulers be' (Arab proverb). A nation with a great *asabiyah* will choose leaders who are worthy to lead it.

- If you become the strategic leader of an organization with great people in it, you are lucky, for they will draw out the greatness in you. One day you may be able to inspire others in the way that they inspired you.

- Do you have a vision of the greatness in people? The test lies not in your words but whether or not you are becoming more humble as a leader.

Not geniuses, but average men require profound stimulation, incentive towards creative effort, and the nurture of great hopes.

John Collier, British-born author and screenplay writer
(1901–80)

10

DEVELOPING TODAY'S AND TOMORROW'S LEADERS

You are not born a leader, you become one.
Proverb of the Balimbe tribe in West Africa

The seventh function of strategic leadership is to select and train leaders at strategic, operational and team leadership levels. Again, as a strategic leader you should take ownership of that challenge – and it will be no surprise to you that here as elsewhere you should lead from the front.

The position is that we do know how to train team leaders, based on the three circles model – the generic role of leader, though largely through ignorance that hard-won know-how is grossly underused. That is the foundation.

Practice and reflection are the way in which those individuals with an aptitude for leadership at operational and strategic levels prepare themselves – or are prepared – for these roles.

Some chief executives make the mistake of regarding only themselves and their fellow directors as leaders and the rest as managers. Diligent readers of this book will not fall into that fallacy. Indeed, looking even beyond the all-important team leaders, it is possible to see all of your employees as leaders in their own way. That makes you into a 'leader of leaders'.

Few organizations are really geared towards developing to the full the *leadership potential* within them. Sometimes this may be due to the fact that they place little or no premium upon it, assuming either that it is not important or that the conventional management training will provide it. Only the best organizations show real and sustained commitment to selecting and developing their business leaders. Why? Because those organizations know from experience that effective leadership at all levels is essential for their continued success.

A short course on leadership:

> The six most important words: 'I admit I made a mistake.'
>
> The five most important words: 'I am proud of you.'
>
> The four most important words: 'What is your opinion?'
>
> The three most important words: 'If you please.'
>
> The two most important words: 'Thank you.'
>
> The one most important word: 'We.'
>
> And the least important word: 'I.'

As a strategic leader you should ensure that your organization has a strategy for leadership development covering these elements. You should, of course, lead by example, making as sure as possible that you practise what you preach.

I cannot hear what you are saying to me, because what you are doing is shouting at me.

Zulu proverb

Seize opportunities for talking to your managers about leadership, not in an academic sense but what it means to you personally and why you think it important. On a one-to-one basis with your operational leaders, do not hesitate to offer them advice drawn from your own practical wisdom.

In both limited success and failure, there are leadership lessons to be harvested.

CASE STUDY: LEARNING TO LEAD AT YOUR NEW LEVEL

Lieutenant-General Sir Brian Horrocks commanded 13 Corps, a group of armoured divisions, under Montgomery at the crucial battle of Alam Halfa on 31 August 1942, when Rommel made his final attempt to win Egypt. Horrocks's troops took the brunt of the attack and within three days the thrust had been defeated. In his memoirs, *A Full Life* (1960), he recounted this sequel:

> On the day after the battle (Alam Halfa) I was sitting in my headquarters purring with satisfaction. The battle had been won and I had not been mauled in the process. What could be better? Then in came a liaison officer from the Eighth Army headquarters bringing me a letter in Monty's even hand. This is what he said:
>
> > Dear Horrocks,
> >
> > Well done – but you must remember that you are now a corps commander and not a divisional commander…

He went on to list four or five things which I had done wrong, mainly because I had interfered too much with the tasks of my subordinate commanders. The purring stopped abruptly. Perhaps I wasn't quite such a heaven-sent general after all. But the more I thought over the battle, the more I realized that Monty was right. So I rang him up and said, 'Thank you very much.'

I mention this because Montgomery was one of the few commanders who tried to train the people who worked under him. Who else, on the day after his first major victory, which had altered the whole complexion of the war in the Middle East, would have taken the trouble to write a letter like this in his own hand to one of his subordinate commanders?

Not long after the following battle at Alamein, while preparing for the final offensive in Tunisia, Horrocks was gravely wounded while in the forward area. After a year in hospital, soon after D-Day, he took command of 30 Corps on the Normandy beaches – once more under Montgomery – and put into practice the lessons he had learned at Alam Halfa.

What Montgomery was doing, as we can all recognize, amounted to 'on-the-job' training in strategic leadership for one of his senior operational leaders now in a strategic leadership role. Hedged between two great battles only days apart, Montgomery both found the time to do it – time management – and did so directly and effectively. Horrocks, for his part, had great respect for Montgomery – 'He was obviously a complete master of his craft, the craft of war' – and he had the humility to see that he had much to learn about giving his divisional commanders direction and freedom.

Development is always self-development. Nothing could be more absurd than for an enterprise to assume responsibility for the development of a person.

Peter Drucker

CHECKLIST: DEVELOPING TODAY'S AND TOMORROW'S LEADERS

	Yes	No
1. Do you have a clear strategy for developing leadership at every level?		
2. When selecting people for management jobs, do you assess them in terms of their leadership abilities (task, team and individual) and the associated qualities of personality and character?		

3. Are appointed team leaders given a minimum of two days of leadership training?
  – always
  – sometimes
  – never		

4. Do you have some system for career development so that future senior leaders broaden their experience and knowledge?		
5. Are all line managers convinced that they are the real leadership trainers, however effective they are in that role?		
6. Is there a specialist 'research and development' team that is keeping the organization and its line managers up to date – and up to the mark?		
7. Has your organizational structure been evolved with good leadership in mind?		
8. Do leaders, actual or potential, realize that they are the ones who 'own' their self-development?		

9. Would you say that there was room for improving the organizational culture or ethos?
  – a great deal
  – some
  – none		

10. Are your top leaders really behind leadership development?
  – whole-heartedly
  – half-heartedly
  – not yet		

KEY POINTS

▨ Good leadership tends to grow naturally in organizations and communities where leadership is esteemed. What you value is what you get. Build a culture and climate that grow leaders naturally.

▨ Your seventh function as a strategic leader is to select and develop leaders for today and tomorrow, especially at operational and team leader levels. Think of yourself as a 'leader of leaders'.

▨ Leadership and learning go hand in hand. Set an example to others by continuously seeking to improve your own performance in the role of strategic leader.

▨ Remember the three circles. You should have a relationship not just with your strategic leadership team as a group but with each individual senior leader on a one-to-one basis. Help them to become effective operational leaders.

▨ Find some oases or wells in the desert of life where you can refresh your own spirit. If you are not inspired, how can you inspire others?

Look well into yourself; there is a source which will always spring up if you will search there.

Marcus Aurelius, Roman emperor (second century AD)

CONCLUSION

"We are to consider our responsibilities, not ourselves. We are to pay regard to our duties of which we are capable, but not our capabilities simply considered." So said William Gladstone, perhaps the most outstanding British prime minister and statesman of the nineteenth century. These wise words remind us that leadership is an other-centred activity, not a self-centred one.

That, indeed, has been the theme of this book. A good part of the journey to becoming an effective strategic leader, I believe, is already behind you once you are clear in your mind what the job entails.

For once you know clearly what others expect from a leader, you can apply yourself with confidence to the lifelong task of developing – or acquiring – the knowledge, skills and personal qualities you need to achieve success.

At any level leadership is a practical art. You learn it by doing it. Really the most that a book like this one can do is to cut down the time that you take to learn by experience. Or, putting it another way, it offers you the opportunity to learn from the experience of others what works and what doesn't work.

To make progress as a leader you need both knowledge of principles – the timeless yet ever timely truths about leadership – and plenty of experience, preferably in more than one field and at more than one level. It is when the sparks jump between principles and practice, theory and experience, that learning takes place. Then you will find yourself continually moving forwards and upwards on the path of leadership.

Lastly, I hope that you will have found some seeds of inspiration in these pages. For if you are inspired you will find it within your power to inspire others.

> Friend, you have read enough,
> If you desire still more,
> Then be the odyssey yourself,
> And all that it stands for.
>
> *From a seventeenth century German poem*

INDEX

NB: page numbers in *italic* indicate figures or tables